D0672153

Alvin Zander

groups at work

Jossey-Bass Publishers
San Francisco • Washington • London • 1977

GROUPS AT WORK
Unresolved Issues in the Study of Organizations
by Alvin Zander

615 Montgomery Street
San Francisco, California 94111
&
Jossey-Bass Limited
28 Banner Street
London EC1Y 8QE

Library of Congress Catalogue Card Number LC 77-82918

International Standard Book Number ISBN 0-87589-347-3

Manufactured in the United States of America

JACKET DESIGN BY WILLI BAUM

FIRST EDITION

Code 7748

The Jossey-Bass
Social and
Behavioral Science Series

Preface

A rich body of organized knowledge has developed in the past few decades from research on the psychology of groups and organizations. Some of this work has appealed to organizational leaders who modified policies and procedures within their units so these units might benefit from this store of ideas. Accordingly, we have seen active interest by both scholars and practitioners in such issues as the grounds on which the authority of managers is based, the way managers are expected to act toward colleagues, the methods members use in reaching decisions for their organization, the nature and source of organizational rules, and the procedures for reducing conflict between groups. Scientists and practitioners alike are pleased with the growth in collaboration between theory and application and are confident it will continue.

This growth, however, is exceedingly slow, for several familiar reasons. One is that it takes many months for a social scientist to finish an empirical study or program of research; a practical person is needed to hear about and understand the results; and an official must plan, introduce, and implement a change in his organization. Another reason for slow growth, and an important one in my view, is the preference of scientists to work on familiar problems rather than on ones unexplainable by accepted theories. This working and reworking of old theories results in slower scientific and practical progress than if scientists more often investigated completely new subjects.

And times change. The problems that stimulated research on groups to date are no longer as urgent as they once were. Indeed, many of the current topics of research first attracted the attention of behavioral scientists when the world had to be "saved for democracy," when Senator Joseph McCarthy's actions inspired fears of being a nonconformist, and when labor unions in corporations first provided a means for workers to counteract the social power of management. These still are crucial issues, to be sure, but many social scientists have not yet recognized that there are now new problems "out there" worthy of investigation. These new problems arise because changes in society and technology alter the environments for organizations. In the last ten years society has developed new laws, values, customs, and fashions that impinge on the ways a group acts; technology has created dilemmas about the wisest use of computers, communication, transportation, energy, carcinogenic materials, and medicines. Such issues have an impact on how an organization performs.

Perhaps a behavioral scientist could best comprehend the current need for research if he were to work for a while as an administrator in a sizable organization. In such a position he would observe events he would want to understand; but, because these events have received little study, he would not be able to explain them sensibly through his store of established information. Examples of such questions include: Why is it so difficult to expel a member nowadays? What is the reason for secrecy in an organization? Why is a modern manager met by abrasive behavior from subordinates? Why are some groups havens of pleasantness, while others distinctly are not? Why do groups set such high goals? How can members improve the efficiency of meetings? How do organizations respond to the rising tide of regulations that limit their actions?

Questions like these interest me because, after years of research and teaching in group behavior, I became an administrator and have seen colleagues attempting to deal with such issues. When I was asked for expert advice, I had little to offer. I realized that many interesting and central problems in group life have been neglected by students of groups, and I found myself wondering why.

One reason has already been implied: Investigators are not aware of these topics because the scientists are busy in the laboratory or classroom and such settings do not provide opportunities to observe group occurrences that characterize formal organizations or to develop a desire to understand them. Questions like those just noted do not suggest themselves, furthermore, as obvious extensions of current theories because there is a relentless logic in building a theory that gradually leads a researcher to study smaller and smaller issues that are more and more removed from the phenomena that initially inspired the theory. Research under these circumstances becomes neater and more restricted.

Another reason is that a problem may be well known, and recognized as a feasible candidate for research, but it is not an urgent or fashionable topic in the eyes of other investigators, those who edit journals, and those who provide funds to support research. Or, the problem may be familiar but ignored because there are no preliminary data about the matter; reliable measures cannot be made of the phenomena; the problem is not properly stated; ethical restrictions exist; or the project is too costly in time, energy, and number of subjects. The issue, in brief, is not researchable.

It is easy to see, in contrast, why other topics are researched. These are problems in which research is feasible, success probable, and support available. The chapters in this book describe a number of seldom-studied problems in work groups. Some may believe these do not warrant investigation. The purpose of *Groups at Work,* however, is to generate interest among researchers because these matters merit careful study, can be researched, would improve our basic knowledge about organizations, and would be interesting to work on. Above all, they might broaden the vision of practitioners and scholars who have worked for years, over and over, on the same aspects of group dynamics while many equally fascinating subjects have been ignored.

In each chapter I describe a typical situation in an organization and provide a framework for thinking about what is going on. It is too pretentious to call these statements theories, even preliminary ones, but they are orderly comments about matters worthy of further practical thought and more careful research. A dominant theme in these chapters is that a group as a unit is an important stimulus and responsibility for members. They often react to it as a unit because they are interested in its successes, its failures, its reputation, and its growth. There is a need to recognize that members work for and develop hopes for their group as such, temporarily putting their own personal dispositions aside, but most of us have long neglected that opportunity for research.

Chapter One first appeared as an article in *Human Relations* in 1976, and many of the ideas in Chapter Four were originally presented at a conference on the use of small groups in national development held at the East-West Communication Institute in 1974 (Chu, Rahim, and Kincaid, 1976). All the chapters are based on notes I jotted while watching events around me in meetings and offices, as an administrator in a large organization, or while thinking about the relevance of group research for explaining such happenings.

Ann Arbor, Michigan
August 1977

ALVIN ZANDER

Contents

The Author

Alvin Zander is Associate Vice-President for Research at the University of Michigan, a position he has held since 1973. He joined the Research Center for Group Dynamics, part of the Institute for Social Research at the University of Michigan, in 1947, and has been its director since 1959.

Zander earned the bachelor's degree in general science (1936), the master's degree in public health (1937), and the doctor's degree in psychology (1942)—all at the University of Michigan. He developed an interest in group behavior while employed as a graduate student during the Great Depression helping small towns develop social services that they could not afford to hire from professionals. After a postdoctoral year with Kurt Lewin at the University of Iowa (1942) and nearly three years as a clinical psychologist and a commissioned officer in the U.S. Public Health Service during World War II, Zander returned to the University of Michigan.

Zander has done research on the relations among persons who differ in their ability to influence others, the impact of group membership on a person's self-regard, the nature of identification between persons, the sources of members' motivation to help their group succeed, and the origins of a group's goals. He is coauthor of *Group Dynamics Research and Theory* (1968) and has published the results of a program of investigations in *Motives and Goals in Groups* (1971).

This book is dedicated, with affection and admiration,
to the present and past staff members of
the Research Center for Group Dynamics

Groups at Work

Unresolved Issues in the Study of Organizations

Chapter One

Recruiting and Removing Members

In the computing room of a large organization, the man on the night shift in charge of the main machine had demonstrated that he was thoroughly unreliable. He often did not show up for work, gave phony excuses for his absences, and expected others to substitute for him on a moment's notice. He was criticized a number of times, in writing, by his supervisor for his undependability, but the supervisor had no authority to take more drastic measures. After a year and a half of repeated no-shows, the employee was asked to stay away from work but was not removed from the payroll. Many meetings followed: by the executive committee of the organization, by the staff of the computing department, by a committee appointed to examine the matter, and by a group of coworkers who objected to the favoritism he had received. There were also endless interviews with the worker, his colleagues, and an amateur lawyer who "defended" his client before many groups. Thus, hundreds of working hours were spent deciding whether the man should be fired. Finally, he was asked to resign. Instead, he simply disappeared.

This is not an isolated instance. Millions of citizens were amazed recently at the millions of dollars and millions of hours devoted to deciding whether the president of this nation should be removed from office. And frequently there are news stories about workers, students, scientists, or policemen who complain they have been dismissed without just cause, and a court holds up the dismissal until hearings have been conducted. Even when expulsion of an unwanted person is easy, because the expellers have enough power to fire anyone they dislike, those in positions of power may feel the need to legitimize their "personnel action" by extracting a confession from the victim or by publicizing the reasons for the exclusion. The book *Gulag Archipelago* (1973) reveals that in some places such justifications can be pretty elaborate, and unjust.

The ushering of members to the outside of a group is often a severe source of strain for all involved. Just as unpleasant, however, is the friction that can arise when a group recruits new members for its roster. Potential candidates are screened, studied, and sorted in order to find an appropriate individual, and tension develops if an applicant is thought by some to be unfairly favored or ignored. Moreover, clubs, companies, and colleges are often pressed by advocates to favor the admission of specific candidates and are damned if they do and damned if they do not.

Dropping members and finding new ones are the most critical processes for a group's continued existence. Each group, or some designated part, must decide which persons, if any, will be asked to depart, who will be invited to stay, and who will be welcome to enter. Despite the importance of these transactions, they have received remarkably little examination beyond anecdotes and descriptive data. This chapter will develop a preliminary understanding of the intake and outgo of members and direct special attention to the reasons why removing and recruiting members may be conducted in ways that are (or are not) in the best interests of all concerned.

Almost all the writing about arranged departures and arrivals of a group's members has been directed to the feelings of the target persons. For example, the removee's loss of self-esteem, mental health, or well-being, not to mention her* loss of money, has been emphasized. Or, a recruit's initial reasons for joining a group and her satisfaction in doing so have received attention. Our concern, in contrast, is group-centered; enrolling and disenrolling members will be considered processes that are performed by the group for the good of the group.

The relevant research into removing and inducting members and past research on group behavior known to me suggest that several kinds of steps are typically taken in organizations in regard to enrolling and disenrolling members. These steps will be presented in the form of *assumptions*; each assumption will introduce related information and speculation. The assumptions, and a number of derivations, called hypotheses, are phrased so they can be linked to concepts that have been used previously in the study of groups—concepts such as group cohesiveness, social pressures, rejection of deviant members, membership motives, and goals of groups.

Removing Members

Assumption: Members of a group decide on conditions which, through the actions of colleagues, must not be allowed to develop in that unit.

For a group to exist and give its members some sense of accomplishment, the participants regularize relationships among

* The traditional use of the masculine pronouns *he* and *his* has not yet been superseded by convenient, generally accepted pronouns that also mean *she* and *her*. To avoid the implied sexism of using only *he* and *his,* I have alternated between masculine and feminine pronouns throughout the book. *She* and *her* should be understood to apply equally to *he* and *his,* and vice versa.

themselves, parts, and activities. These regularizing efforts require joint planning and more or less explicit decisions—the more complex the social unit, the more these agreements tend to be both precise and public. When firm understandings of appropriate conditions in a group are reached, they are often expressed in terms of negative injunctions, that is, in terms of what shall not be allowed or tolerated instead of what shall be approved or welcomed.

A person has fewer excuses for failing a negative injunction than for failing an affirmative injunction, because what should *not* be done can be precisely put and monitored, whereas what ought to be done is open-ended and hard to monitor. Thus liability depends on whether actions within a group have had undesirable consequences, not on whether they failed to do good. To give an example, critics of an ethical code published by a pharmaceutical manufacturers' association view it as a weak statement because most of the code contains rather bland platitudes about the good things a drug company should do. The code would have more impact on the drug companies, say the critics, if it described what a drug maker should *not* do. As another example, eight of the Bible's ten commandments are stated as negatives; that is, as "thou shalt not." And labor-management contracts are richly supplied with barriers to certain actions because each side wants to evaluate accurately the opposition's actions by employing clear criteria.

Six of the unwanted conditions in a group are worth noting: (1) embarrassment over the group's poor performance; (2) inappropriate size of the group—a loss of members when that is not desirable or an excess of members when they are not needed; (3) insufficient supply of persons who have the necessary talent, involvement, and experience, so the group cannot do what it must; (4) inadequate collaboration or excessive conflict among parts of the group; (5) inadequate procedures for accomplishing its task; and (6) unfavorable relations with agents who place pressure on the group, attack it, or interfere with its functioning.

Some groups—college faculties, psychotherapy groups, creative crews in research or writing—are fairly tolerant of those who transgress their injunctions. Other groups—work groups, religious bodies, communes, professional societies, military units, fraternities, ward teams in a hospital—are stricter in demanding adherence. The following assumptions are more relevant to this second group than to the former:

Assumption: The unattractiveness of a given member of a group in the eyes of his colleagues is determined by the negative value of his recent actions and the perceived probability that he will display these actions in the future.

The negative value of an act by a member is a function of the act's significance to the group and the degree it is prohibited there. There are many examples of members' acts that lead to rejection by some organization or other. According to Caplow and McGee (1958), college professors have been released for a quarrelsome disposition, immaturity, and unacceptable political beliefs. College students have been expelled for poor schoolwork, cheating, drinking, gambling, smoking, wearing shorts, driving an automobile in the college town, and breaking rules of sexual propriety. In fraternities and sororities, members are rejected if their values are not those of the other members (Scott, 1965). In the American Psychological Association, members can be dismissed for violation of ethical standards, for committing a felony, or for actions that are a threat to the public. In the American Medical Association, physicians can be discharged from their respective county medical societies for alcoholism, use of drugs, performing an improper abortion, or illegal behavior (Derbyshire, 1974). In a factory, members who will not exert themselves may be fired. Certain actions by certain members, then, are more repulsive under certain conditions than under others.

The severity of any negative action by a group's member is weighed and judged as to whether he will repeat it, how often, and to what degree. This perceived probability will be greater if the member displays such characteristics as engaging in the unwanted behavior for some time, not being able to drop it from his repertoire, being aware that his actions are damaging to the group and yet persisting in such actions, or performing a large (rather than a limited) variety of unpleasant acts. And the perceived probability will be inaccurate if the group makes incorrect estimates of these matters because of poor information or unsound guesses about the member's future behavior.

Thus, an unfavorable action by a group member may signal that this action is likely to recur in the future and makes the member more unattractive to the group, which leads to a third assumption:

Assumption: As a participant in a group becomes more unattractive to her colleagues, the group is more willing to designate her as not a member.

A *group* is a collection of individuals who are interdependent to some degree (Cartwright and Zander, 1968a). A *member,* according to this definition, depends on the group for attainment of consequences she values, such as income, sense of accomplishment, pride in group, affiliation with others, social power, and protection. By the same token, such a collection of individuals depends on each member so the group can move toward achievement of its purposes. The point to make now is that a group can remove a member by arranging things so the rejected one can no longer depend on the group, and the group can no longer depend on the member—the conditions of belonging are abolished.

In an essay about what he calls "degradation ceremonies," Garfinkel (1956, p. 423) lists eight steps or stages that must be passed in order successfully to denounce a person who deserves to be denounced. The last step is: "Finally, the denounced person must be ritually separated from a place in the legitimate order; that is, he must be defined as standing at a place opposed to it. He must be placed 'outside,' he must be made 'strange.' " Removal of a member from his group may seldom be a ritual or a ceremony, but there are subtle distinctions among the verbs used in various settings to describe the process of removal: expel, discharge, dismiss, disenroll, denounce, impeach, excommunicate, reject, release, fire, ostracize, terminate, layoff, RIF, let go, pink slip, and can.

Our emphasis is on the negative evaluation of a rejectee, even though an expelled member may have attractive qualities that are outweighed by his undesirable attributes. The old basketball player who is released, even though he is still as good a player as a new recruit, is not of interest here if he is let go merely because the manager believes it will be wiser in the long run to go with youth than to rely on experience, and if the number of players the manager may keep on the team's roster is limited. The old player's skills are not disparaged by his release; only his age is disparaged, an attribute the player cannot change (Snoek, 1962).

Some ways a member is rendered unable to remain in his group are clear enough: not giving him a salary check, removing his uniform and badge, not letting him have a workplace, not inviting him to meetings, or not sending him messages from headquarters. Other ways are more variable and serve as deprivations so the focal person will voluntarily resign: ignoring him, giving him little work or trivial assignments, or advising him to find a new job or enter a new field. Still other ways are more subtle. Unwanted professors are "sold down the river," according to Caplow and McGee (1958) by secretly arranging job offers for them. This gambit is also used by the Federal Civil Service, and its effect may be hastened by giving a poor worker excellent performance-appraisal ratings so other organizations will want her. An unattractive member may be given a "lost elephant post," one that isolates her from the rest of her colleagues (Huenefeld, 1970), or distant agencies may be invited to make use of her services in the hope that she will gradually drift away to their side (Sills, 1957). A not uncommon practice, if all else fails, is to declare that the job filled by the unwelcome member is no longer needed in the organization, which means that the current occupant of the post is no longer needed as well.

It is striking how little is known about why organizations dispense with colleagues. Many companies conduct exit interviews with people who are leaving, but the reasons exmembers give after they have been asked to depart, or have decided to leave without prompting, are inadequate and biased (Ross and Zander, 1957). Research has to be done on group members in which relevant data are collected about them at one time and these data later compared for those persons who have left and for those who have not. Research is also needed on the nature of the decisions that lead a group to remove one of its members.

Assumption: The tendency of group members to reject an unattractive colleague may be strengthened or weakened by conditions other than those that initially caused his unattractiveness.

There is much evidence that considerations beyond a member's mere repulsiveness determine whether he is dismissed, and some of these considerations serve to *increase* the number of removals from a group. Most common, of course, are forms of discrimination; a participant is removed for reasons other than just cause. In a large university, 180 persons were discharged from noninstructional jobs within one year. Of these people, 56 percent were black and 44 percent were white, 54 percent were women and 46 percent were men. Is it likely that the blacks and the women were more unattractive? Of 36 faculty members whose dismissals were studied by Caplow and McGee (1958) all but two were assistant professors. Are assistant professors consistently the most unattractive members of the faculty? Sometimes, incompetent members are protected by their peers. For example, the number of physicians released from the staffs of hospitals throughout the country, according to information provided by Derbyshire (1974), increased dramatically when the courts ruled that a hospital would be held accountable for any professional act performed by a doctor within its walls. It seems unlikely that a number of doctors suddenly became unattractive at the moment this new rule was passed. Clearly, doctors had been overlooking inept practices rather than reporting them. Poorly performing organizations typically release more members than succeeding organizations do—this is demonstrated at the end of a professional sports season, when losing teams rid themselves of managers and players while winning teams leave well enough alone. Hamblin (1958) reported that groups do not change leaders when things are running smoothly but do when a group's performance falters.

Organizations often invent procedures or customs that make it easy to remove members when the time arrives. Examples are granting a degree, graduation, limit to term of eligibility, probation in hiring, up-or-out policy, and forced retirement from work. An especially colorful example of such dispersal was the *lustrum,* which was held every five years throughout the Holy Roman Empire. Noses were counted by an official *censor,* and citizens whose behavior made them undesirable in a community were exiled.

There are also states of affairs in organizations that *inhibit* the rate of dismissals. Among medical doctors there is what Derbyshire (1974) calls "a conspiracy of silence." That is, doctors seldom report information to their local medical society about the unprofessional conduct of another physician, information that might lead to the physician's removal from the society. This unwillingness to tell is apparently based on a misapplication of the ethical standard that one doctor does not speak ill of another doctor in front of a patient. In the present instance, a doctor does not speak ill of a colleague before a colleague, although the malpractice is a medical menace. As a result, reported misbehaviors and instances of malpractice by doctors are much fewer than those which actually occur, based on other channels of information. Appraisal systems are similarly unreliable in government and industry because superiors do not like to give unfavorable ratings to subordinates (Goffman, 1952; Zander and Gyr, 1955) or to communicate unfavorable opinions about a person to that person. The appraised individuals are made to appear less inadequate mainly because it is more convenient to the appraisers to make them appear so. The most potent constraints on the frequency of discharge are the tenure or seniority rules found in most large organizations. We should note that an increase in the removal of members means the organization is actively protecting itself from unattractive members; whereas a decrease in the removal of members who are obviously unattractive means these persons are being protected from the group.

These anecdotes, which illuminate our fourth assumption, suggest that it might be useful to consider several hypotheses that offer (in more or less testable form) statements about matters that increase or inhibit the rate of removals. (We assume the removee is not eager to leave the group.)

Hypothesis: The greater the cohesiveness of a group, the stronger the group's tendency to remove an unattractive member.

This hypothesis has been supported by Festinger, Schachter, and Back (1950) and by the work of Schachter (1951), whose critical experiment has been replicated and supported in seven countries. The *cohesiveness* of a group is defined as the strength of the members' desire to remain members. Observe then that less cohesive groups tend to be more tolerant of unattractive persons. More generally speaking, this hypothesis suggests that members who are particularly involved in the fate of a group are more alert to the threat an unattractive person represents for that group.

Hypothesis: The less just the reason for removing an unattractive member from the group, the weaker the tendency to remove her.

In terms of whether to expel a member, a just procedure is one that gives primary weight to the member's offensive rather than beneficial qualities and follows accepted rules for making an objective appraisal of her. To be unjust, then, is to be biased or dishonest in judging the effect of a member's actions on the group, to judge a member incorrectly, to give her unusual benefit of the doubt, or to break the rules of due process developed within that organization. The point of the hypothesis is that some members (or agents outside the group) are likely to object if, in their view, colleagues are being unfairly judged and removed for reasons other than unattractiveness as we have defined it.

The amount of value placed on justice within a given group may stem from several sources. There is traditional but not universal support in Western society for practices that protect persons from the actions of their group. Civil rights legislation, increasing in detail and coverage year by year, prevents discrimination in firing or hiring. Some laws require that due process be followed when releasing or selecting people (but these laws do not apply to all groups). National associations and local organizations set standards and goals that require fair practice for their attainment. It stands to reason that social pressures on a group toward fairness are more effective if the originators of these pressures have sufficient power to influence members of the group.

Hypothesis: The greater the harm to an unattractive member by removing him from the group, the weaker the tendency to remove him.

As noted, expulsion may hurt the expellee. His loss of self-esteem was discussed by Goffman (1952) and by Cartwright and Zander (1968b), and this loss is greater if the dismissal is based on grounds that are derogatory to him (Snoek, 1962). Removal from a group can mean that the target person is deprived of his job, income, career, status, opportunity to practice a profession, or other things he values along with his membership. Furthermore, removal may expose the member to physical or psychological dangers from which the group has shielded him, and it may foster rejection by other agencies, especially if his discharge is dishonorable and the reason is not concealed from the agencies. Thus, compassion for a potential rejectee is more likely as it is more apparent that dismissal would cause him greater harm.

Hypothesis: If the removal of an unattractive member is harmful to the group, the tendency to remove her is weakened.

An example of this fourth hypothesis is the retention of an unattractive member because dismissing her will make the group look bad (because it is not able to help inept members improve themselves) or will generate conflict between those who support her and those who do not. As a result, some organizations keep members they would prefer to expel. Such a restraint is commonly used in schools, prisons, communes, hospitals, theological seminaries, and religious sects. There is also the possibility that procedures for justifying the dismissal of an unattractive member may be so complicated that it is easier to live with the stress the undesirable member causes than to endure the strain of dismissal hearings.

Hypothesis: If removing an unattractive member decreases valued contributions he makes to the group, the tendency to remove him is weaker.

An unattractive person's behavior may be excused or overlooked because he has done things in behalf of that organization that outweigh his faults. Hollander (1961) describes such a person as having "idiosyncrasy credit"; that is, he is allowed to be deviant because previously he made valuable contributions to the organization.

Hypothesis: If removing an unattractive member exposes the group to retaliation by the rejectee or her supporters, the tendency to remove her is weaker.

When such retaliation is feared, an unwanted member may be allowed to resign, thereby saving herself, and the organization, from backlash. This privilege is often granted to prestigious members. For example, a member of a labor union is not lightly dismissed, nor is a person who can readily organize a cohort of supporters, such as a popular young professor who calls on students to help her keep her job.

Voluntary Departure. Students of personnel practices often remark that an individual resigns when his group does not appreciate or recognize him or provide him with satisfaction (Ross and Zander, 1957). A member who is unwelcome probably senses that fact and may therefore quit before he is fired. It is not unusual for a business firm to lose 35 to 50 percent of its rank and file workers each year. (The proportion of losses at the managerial levels is much lower.) The ideas advanced earlier are best suited perhaps to the behavior of a person who will not or cannot leave an organization, even though he is not wanted, because he has training that is especially suited to that group, more need for the group, or more status in the group.

Voluntary departures are no doubt more frequent than dismissals. In a study of professors, for example, only 17 percent were dismissed; of the rest, 57 percent resigned, 16 percent retired, and 10 percent died (Caplow and McGee, 1958). It is believed that many who resigned did so because they were urged to leave, although among the reasons the professors gave were things not always going well, discord within their departments, other interests, personal reasons, and unbeatable offers from other schools.

Consequences of Rejection. We noted that it is not pleasant to be dropped from group membership, especially if one leaves under duress. Goffman (1952) wrote with great insight, based on his own observations, about the "destruction" of a rejectee's self-concept because a forced removal reveals to him that his former colleagues think he is inept. It is also possible that departure of an unwanted person may initiate "a time of healing" within a group and allow a recovery of the efficiency and coordination which had been lost during the presence of the departed one.

Whatever the personal consequences of removal may be, and they are not all bad, organizations commonly try to reduce the negative ones. The target person may be helped to find a new job. The reasons for her dismissal may be kept from others or not accurately reported to them. She may be allowed to save face by such ways as noted by Goffman and by Clark (1960): providing her a new view of herself, offering her a different social position or another chance, and letting her have an emotional catharsis. Clearly, the motivation here is sympathy and care for the individual's health rather than adherence to a code of civil rights.

Recruiting Members

To speculate sensibly about recruitment and what causes it to go one way rather than another, we should discuss an assumption that is the inverse of the first assumption in this chapter.

Assumption: Members of a group decide on conditions which, through the actions of members, should be developed in that unit.

As we discussed, groups do not state their standards exclusively in the form of shall nots. Often they express the standards as desired outcomes, usually in less precise terms than those used to express negative injunctions. Examples of desired group conditions include attaining pride in the group as a result of its performance on a task, maintaining optimal size of the group, securing members who have talents for the work to be done, encouraging smooth collaboration instead of friction among members, developing effective procedures for the group's work, and fostering useful interactions with agents outside the group.

Assumption: The attractiveness of an individual in the eyes of group members is determined by the positive value of his particular acts or attributes and the probability that he will reveal these qualities in the future.

Personal qualities a group might value in a member include skill, ability, talent, money, good name, experience, training, physical attractiveness, willingness to work, or even lack of undesirable attributes.

Some organizations take great care in observing and measuring the characteristics of potential members. The candidates are given tests and individual interviews or tryouts, and the spouse may be examined. Search committees in colleges, churches, business firms, and government agencies spend endless hours sorting and selecting potential candidates. Indeed, these tasks can become so onerous that a firm of recruiters may be hired to do them. Because the tests are sometimes unreliable and the results sometimes misused, there has been a proliferation of rules, even laws, concerning who can measure such things and how, especially in federal agencies. And because of the weaknesses in many testing programs, counselors may advise job applicants to give incorrect answers when taking the tests so that the results will be meaningless and cannot be used to determine the testee's fate (Whyte, 1956).

There are associations in which a potential member does not need many qualities to be attractive; it is enough if she has the initiation fee, a vote, legs that can help in a demonstration, a marinated liver, or a soul to be saved. In other kinds of groups, the attractiveness of a potential member almost entirely depends on the fact that she needs the group or that the group will do her good—members welcome the chance to help her.

Assumption: An individual who is more attractive to those in a group is more likely to be invited to become a member.

An invitation extended to an outsider, unlike the removal of an insider, requires assent by the invited one. That is, he must be asked and he must accept—unless, of course, he is being put into prison or being drafted into the army. In a study of participants in a voluntary agency, it was observed that 90 percent had been asked

to join, whereas only 10 percent had applied for membership on their own initiative. Among those who were recruited, 52 percent applied at the request of a friend, 20 percent at the request of a community member, and 18 percent through the invitation of a coworker (Sills, 1957).

Again, in contrast to removing, when a group is recruiting, members must convince a potential recruit that he will benefit from joining; these appeals are made in various ways. The newcomer is shown that the group's programs are important to the community of which he is a part and he will presumably help that community by joining (Toch, 1965). He is shown that the group provides opportunities he values, such as a chance to use his skills, to practice his profession, to accomplish personal goals, to have fun, to be wanted, to earn money, to have security, to be personally changed in some way, or to escape (Anderson, 1947; Sills, 1957; Scott, 1965). He is shown that the group contains members who will be compatible with him and who presumably, therefore, will cooperate with him (Newcomb, 1961; Scott, 1965). He is told that the organization will defend or protect him against fearful conditions—this approach is used by the Ku Klux Klan, the Communist party, the John Birch Society, unions, and fundamentalist churches. The recruit is gently involved in the group by being asked to do a small job for it, in the hope that the minor involvement will convince him that there are appealing qualities in the group and that he would like permanently to join the group (Huenefeld, 1970). And taking a part in an organization's activities or programs may make the participant realize that he will benefit from full-fledged membership—he can then be further socialized until he deeply depends upon that unit (Katz, 1964; Coulter and Taft, 1973; Whyte, 1974). Or, he is within a group that provides help for another group, and as a result (it is hoped) he decides to join the group needing help (Huenefeld, 1970).

Sometimes it is necessary for a group to be convinced about the virtues of a potential candidate. The decision makers accordingly must be told how and why the potential member "is like us" or "will benefit us" or how "we will benefit him." The permeability of the membrane that divides an organization from outsiders partly determines the amount of care taken in choosing new recruits. A group with a thin boundary (a group anyone can join), such as a social movement, will be less careful, though perhaps not less active, in getting people to sign up. A group with a thick boundary (only special people can join), like a professional association or an elite club, will be extremely careful in their recruitment. Kanter (1972) observed that communes differ in their readiness to accept new members. Those that a person joins to escape the world are easy to penetrate, but those a person joins to save the world are harder to get into.

Assumption: The tendency of group members to enroll an attractive individual may be strengthened or weakened by conditions other than those that initially caused his attractiveness.

Faults in recruiting are not as dramatic as those in expelling, so they do not get as much attention. Yet one hears accounts that support this assumption. Often these stories describe discriminatory hiring practices because members of minority groups, or women, have not been given adequate consideration for the openings. Truly, some persons are hired for reasons that do not strike one as first class. Quinn, Tabor, and Gordon (1968) examined the criteria recruiters said they used when selecting new members for business firms. Of those interviewed, 98 percent reported that they used a "good clean-cut appearance" to evaluate managerial candidates; 69 percent used "looking like a manager" as an evaluative criterion. Bowman (1962) found that "having a good appearance" ranked above a college education, loyalty, and inventiveness. Other studies have reported that fat people, or short ones, are seldom chosen as managers.

School superintendents often feel pressure to hire one teacher rather than another, such as the mayor's daughter (Gross, Mason, and McEachern, 1958), and a southern university president, who was warned against appointing members of minority groups, was fired when he ignored the warning. A tight budget limits the hiring of people in some organizations, whereas other organizations, especially colleges, military units, and nursing staffs, cannot get enough people today. Within a large organization, moreover, particular groups may be given more support by higher officials and allowed to do more recruiting. Yet the favored groups may not be the most critical for the fate of the larger entity, and thus the recruited persons may not in fact be the most attractive. Who decides who can or cannot recruit, and why? There are no data on that question.

There are reasons, however, that the most attractive persons are (or are not) the ones who are actually recruited. Some of these reasons are open to study and are stated here in the form of hypotheses, as before.

Hypothesis: The greater the cohesiveness of a group, the more the member prefers an attractive recruit.

The idea in this hypothesis is that members who are more attracted to membership and more concerned about the fate of their group, because the group is an important means for their attaining valued ends, will be more eager to bring promising candidates into the unit. To illustrate, the officers of a United Fund executive board, because they were more responsible for the success of the agency, were more interested in the quality of the volunteers brought in to help the fund than were the members who were less responsible for the board's success (Zander, Forward, and Albert, 1969). The hypothesis also implies that groups with less cohesiveness are not as likely to weigh the attractiveness of new members; thus, less attractive persons are quite recruitable in such a group.

It follows that an individual's appeal will be based on factors that are important to current members. That is, a person who needs emotional support from others will be more desirable if members see their group as a provider of such support; an able and vigorous individual will be more desirable if the members are concerned with group success on a motor task; or a socially powerful person will be more desirable if the members are striving to have their group generate changes in society. Perhaps this is a special version of the way in which birds of a feather flock together (Scott, 1965).

Hypothesis: Individuals who are considered more able to benefit from membership in the group are more likely to be invited to join the group.

As noted, the prime purpose of some organizations—churches, political parties, social movements, self-improvement societies, communes—is to help individual members as persons. The neophyte is taken in not because of what she can do for the group but because of what the group can do for her. Goal-directed organizations do not neglect this member-improvement purpose, as evidenced by the company that hires the son of a manager's friend because on-the-job experience will help the son grow up or recruits an untrained young person in order to give him a chance.

Hypothesis: A failing group, in contrast to a succeeding one, is more likely to seek and accept new members.

One aspect of this hypothesis was mentioned in passing. Quite commonly, members in a successful group "let well enough alone" and do not recruit new persons. In a failing group, in contrast, there is an obvious need for improvement and this often can be best developed by finding new members, especially ones with qualities that will help the group improve. Festinger, Riecken, and Schachter (1956) described religious sects that engaged in active proselytizing only after their sect had failed and its future was threatened.

Hypothesis: As a group's members place more weight on the importance of justice, they are more disposed to choose a recruit on grounds of merit rather than other attributes.

A recent editorial about recruiting in *Science* states: "If this principle [merit] is lost, mediocrity becomes inevitable" (Denny, 1974). A just group seeks to provide equal treatment for all and develops a procedure (due process) to ensure that justice is met. Justice also demands that group members search for reasons that justify any departure from equal treatment for all. We noted that there can be many reasons for fairness in an organization, not the least of which is the value placed on justice itself in the social environment of the group.

Due process in recruiting is, in some cases, determined by a set of rules jointly developed by a number of organizations. The recruitment of athletes by colleges, for example, is done in accordance with strict regulations that keep one school from obtaining an unfair advantage in talent over another. The recruitment of college players for professional teams is likewise governed by a set of ethics (not always honored), as is the selection of interns by hospitals and staff members by senators and representatives.

Hypothesis: The stronger the cohesiveness of a group, the more members will adhere to objective recruiting procedures.

Ordinarily, stronger cohesiveness enhances adherence to whatever norms exist in a group concerning recruitment of members (Cartwright and Zander, 1968a). But a prior hypothesis has suggested that greater group cohesiveness engenders stronger attention to the attractiveness (merit) of potential recruits. Both that hypothesis and this one imply therefore that stronger cohesiveness leads to more careful use of due process in recruiting. Thus, the intention to recruit attractive persons, and to be more just in doing so, is probably better developed in more cohesive units. It may be, then, that unjust recruiting is more often allowed (or even encouraged) in groups with low cohesiveness, at least in today's climate.

Finally, several types of restraints on recruiting are worth noting. One is the unwillingness of members to seek additions to their group because new members must be broken in. For example, members of a social-action group that investigates the ethical practices of business firms often talked about the need for more members to share their work load yet made no move to find recruits and did not welcome persons who applied for membership. A small club quit seeking new members after several invitees refused an invitation to join, and a research unit stopped searching for additions to its staff because the searching took away too much time from research.

Successful Recruiting. Some groups are more successful in obtaining recruits, and some recruitment practices work better than others. Published comments about how to obtain new members advocate procedures that are surprisingly similar to those used in selling or in getting people to change their minds. Writings about recruiting are devoted mainly to the reasons individuals give for accepting an invitation to join a group or for applying to join it. These issues are central in work by Schachter (1951); Jackson (1959); Snoek (1962); Smith (1966); Cartwright and Zander (1968a); and Zygmunt (1972).

In a study in which rural people were asked to take part in groups devoted to improving agriculture and rural life, Anderson (1947) indicated that groups have more success if the whole family is invited to join, and youth clubs maintain that membership campaigns are most effective if newcomers are invited by friends who already are members. The point is that individuals will be more comfortable in an unfamiliar setting if they are brought into it by people they know in the group. Anderson also believes that the invitation is most effective if it is first offered to the individual who is the decision maker of the family, usually the mother. Accordingly, a group might ask a manager, teacher, minister, or other official to put in a good word about the group to the person they want to join. Huenefeld advocates that a political campaign recruit persons in pairs because each person can give support to the other when needed.

Many agencies establish procedures, or even ceremonies, that lead to membership at an established time. These procedures have familiar names: initiation, confirmation, investiture, entrance, licensing, inauguration, rite de passage, swearing in, and the like. In Norway, a person is a full-fledged member of the Lutheran church as soon as she or he is born.

Consequences of Recruitment. An organization recruits new blood to improve itself, but this improvement does not always happen. Caplow and McGee (1958) asserted that a professor did not work out well because he was not thoroughly investigated prior to his hiring or undue weight was given to matters other than his merit. Similarly, Slesinger (1961) reported that the management levels in government agencies are often burdened with mediocre persons because poor recruiting practices, along with the protection provided by civil service, let less capable people drift to the top. Some groups get an appealing flavor because they include lost souls, fanatics, or disturbed people. Kanter's review (1972) of old and new communes and the book *The True Believer* by Eric Hoffer (1951) sympathetically describe such groups and their special kinds of members.

Selective recruiting causes an organization to ingest persons who become committed to it and who value their participation there (Aronson and Mills, 1959; Slesinger, 1961; Kanter, 1972). Groups that favor the recruitment of individuals who are "like us" hold their members longer and have more stability (Scott, 1965), partly because the similarity in beliefs and style generate harmony. It is apparent that wise recruiting can be a substitute for internal social control in the sense that people, who are recruited because they know how to behave, do not need to be pressured to conform to the group's standards. Etzioni (1964, p. 68) makes this point in the following paragraph: "All other things being equal, socialization and selectivity can frequently substitute for each other. . . . If the number of potential participants is close to that of actual participants, the degree to which selectivity can be increased is limited and the organization will have to rely on socialization to attain a given level of equality. A very large number of potential participants and a very high degree of selectivity may be required to recruit participants who do not need any socialization at all in order to fulfill organizational requirements."

Summary

The critical processes of dropping members and finding new ones are done by a group for the good of the group. A person is more likely to be removed if he engages in actions that the group has prohibited and if it appears he will continue to display such undesirable ways. Removal of an unattractive member is less likely to occur, however, if the removal will be unfair or cause harm to the person or group. In some organizations, procedures have been developed to prevent unwanted by-products of removing a member.

A person is more likely to be recruited if his acts or attributes promise to strengthen desirable conditions in the group. Such attractive persons are more desirable if the group is highly cohesive, joining the group will help the newcomer, and the members place strong emphasis on being fair and just in their recruiting practices.

Chapter Two

Secrecy Within an Organization

There are many examples of secrecy in workplaces. A large envelope marked *Confidential* arrives in a company's mail. When the envelope is opened, it is discovered that the envelope contains a brief form which shows the new salary for an employee. During a committee meeting the secretary is instructed to keep certain comments out of the minutes and, at the end of the session, is told what deliberations should be made public and what should be concealed. Managers do not tell some things to certain colleagues yet readily report them to others. Many legal, military, religious, or medical agencies deal with private matters all the time and often pledge their members to silence.

Groups at Work

Because of its widespread use, organizational secrecy should be a common subject of study; instead, it has been ignored. True, there has been research into the purposes of communication, the direction or amount of talk within a group, and the effects of free interaction among members, and the questions of why communication is ineffective and how its effectiveness can be improved have been investigated. But such studies are not very pertinent to an understanding of the nature of secrecy. Thus, this chapter will consider the purposes and the consequences of secrecy among group members.

Nature of Secrecy

Secrecy is the intentional concealment of specific information from particular persons. A person is not being secretive if he does not communicate because of an oversight or if he poorly phrases a thought. And secrecy is not unconscious concealment or an unwillingness to talk because of shyness. Secrecy is a *planned* and *overt* set of efforts.

There are numerous ways of practicing secrecy: the special courier, the secret code, scrambled telephonic transmission, the doctored photograph, the envelope fastened with a seal, the "eyes only" on a message, and other devices familiar to students of administration. And there are just as many ways to uncover secrecy, such as code deciphering, illegally opening mail, furtively recording conversations, employing ultrasensitive microphones, wiretapping, tailing suspected persons, photographing from a distance, hypnotizing or drugging those who will not reveal secrets, and establishing social institutions, staffed by special operatives, to uncover concealed matters.

Often a secret is leaked to reveal dishonest practices. Recently there has been an increasing number of exposés in which a member of an organization, on his own initiative, publicly reports wrongdoing within that group. The book *Whistle Blowing* by Nader, Petkas, and Blackwell (1972) gives detailed advice on how best to report hidden unethical practices in an organization and describes many successful (and unsuccessful) revelations in government and industry. And because anyone who "blows a whistle" is subject to reprisal (and this reprisal can be severe), the agency called *The Clearing House for Professional Responsibility* was established to help such exposers; also, legislation that prohibits retribution against any employee who publicly reveals illegal matters in her unit has been proposed. When a secret has been leaked, the guardians of the secret are of course embarrassed and may use various techniques to camouflage their actions. Some common subterfuges are giving out part of the story, placing incorrect emphasis in a message so it will lead attention away from the main topic, claiming special dispensation, denying, forgetting, deleting, obscuring, changing the issue, counterattacking, or even "taking the Fifth."

Obviously both uncovering and keeping secrets can be a complex and nasty business. But in most organizations this business is little more than carefully controlling who knows or learns what. And there are valid reasons for this secrecy, as we shall discover from the assumptions in this chapter.

Assumption: Members of an organization use secrecy to prevent the occurrence of undesirable conditions within that organization.

An example of a potentially undesirable condition is from the testimony of a spokesman for the National Science Foundation during his appearance before a congressional committee that was examining the wisdom of admitting the public to previously closed committee meetings whose purpose was to judge the merit of requests for research funds. "To open the peer review process to public, even congressional scrutiny, could destroy it—because it is based on confidentiality. Good scientists will not make candid—meaning negative—assessments of each other's work if they have to operate in the open" (Culliton, 1975b, p. 535). And again: "Suppose," said one NSF spokesman, "that a rejected applicant knew the identity of the scientists who reviewed and turned down his application. He could write his congressman and challenge their competence. We'd be under great pressure" (Culliton, 1975b, p. 535).

As a second example, several dozen patients in a large hospital all developed similar symptoms of a severe illness within a short period of time, arousing suspicion that these sudden onsets were the work of someone who intended to harm the patients. When reporters requested the names of individuals in particular posts in the hospital, the request was refused "because the reporters would pester these people to death." Finally, some states have laws that forbid anyone who has access to secret information about management's bargains with an employee's union to join that union. In this case the secrecy itself has to be legally protected.

Assumption: A member of a group is more willing to keep specific information secret as he believes more strongly that concealment will prevent undesirable conditions for himself or the organization.

Secrecy is used in many parts of an organization to prevent such unwanted events as (1) ineffective functioning by the collective unit, (2) friction in the interpersonal relations among members, (3) embarrassment for an individual who is the subject of the secret, or (4) self-embarrassment. Let us now consider these four stimuli for secrecy in turn; the conditions under which they are most conducive to secret keeping merit further study.

An organization often uses secrecy to ensure the group's continual functioning. For instance, sometimes secrecy prevents group members from reacting too early to incomplete plans in ways they would be less likely to use when the plans are completely laid out. Thus managers keep quiet about the nature of a potential decision until it is ready for the light of day, a financial budget is not announced until the announcers have finished their work on it, or the plans for a new building are not disseminated until the ideas are well enough defined to benefit from discussion. The rule may be that vaguer plans generate greater desire for secrecy (or greater fear of exposure).

Another frequent purpose for withholding information from

a group is to prevent the overloading of communication channels that can occur when more information than can be grasped, or can be used at the moment, is available. To simplify what is passed along, some information is deliberately held back. Perhaps this occurs more often when the information is unpleasant or highly technical.

Also, a poor performance by an organization, whether it be in terms of production, profit, or reputation, will be kept from members when possible, so that the members do not develop a low opinion of their organization or lose interest in its fate. And secrecy is commonly used to protect a group from developing a competitive disadvantage with other bodies; that is, a company may have trade secrets and so make every effort, supported by law, to protect them from being learned by rival firms. The greater the rivalry, we might guess, the more the secrecy.

Finally, information about a company is often concealed from employees because "it is not in the best interest of the firm to reveal it." A corporation conceals such matters as its productivity, profits, taxes, gifts to politicians, bribes to brokers, plans for new products, complaints by customers, lawsuits, toxic effects of its products, and dishonest descriptions of these adverse effects. (Many of these examples are legally concealment, not secrecy. Concealment is the withholding of something one knows and which, in duty, one is bound to reveal—in honesty and good faith the facts ought to be communicated. Concealment is thus equivalent to deceit, evasion, omission, or suppression; Leedes and Gilbert, 1961.)

There are instances in which it is wise to conceal information within an organization because revelation of it might cause the second undesirable condition: hostility between individuals or groups. An administrator will ordinarily keep it quiet when one person derogates another individual in her hearing, and she will seldom say that a given person is, in her eyes, superior to another—even when such a statement might stimulate improvement in the person(s). A manager will also conceal that a set of persons is being paid more than another or is being given more advantages than a comparable set. Personnel departments are famous for sending secret messages about employees to a limited list of recipients. Secrecy in this case circumvents the possibility of social comparisons and resultant hard feelings among those who learn that they are deprived—events personnel workers are taught to dread. It seems likely then that when hostility between parts of an organization already exists, the tendency to use secrecy is greater. Finally, during bargaining between labor and management both sides want secrecy because they wish to keep their plans, the weight of their separate demands, and the compromises they are willing to make unknown to the other side—effective bargaining is thought to depend on hiding information.

This unwillingness of individuals to initiate topics of conversation that might be unpleasant for the recipient and that might arouse him to retaliate has been called the "MUM effect" by Rosen (1970) and Tesser and Rosen (1975). These scholars showed that the MUM effect is a robust phenomenon which occurs in a variety of settings; it explains why most of us dislike delivering bad news.

Specific information about a given person, especially if it is derogatory of him in some way, is often kept a secret. Thomas Jefferson called such secrecy "protection of the innocent." A low appraisal rating, a poor grade in a course, or the reasons for being fired, being demoted, or being suspected of criminal behavior are commonly kept in closed records. This compassionate secrecy is justified on the grounds that one should not do social injury to another, which is why many organizations that have information about individuals in their files are developing guidelines concerning the "rights of privacy."

Often, when a person's opinions are solicited, she is promised that her comments will be kept confidential; this promise is made so the opinion giver will speak as freely as she wishes. Such an assurance is given to referees for the evaluation of articles submitted to professional journals, to those who write letters commenting on a candidate's suitability for a position, to members of review committees who appraise the acceptability of research proposals, or to individuals who apply for employment in an organization. But now the Freedom of Information Act makes it hard to keep promises of confidentiality. For example, many high school teachers refuse to write recommendations for high school students applying to college, according to the experience of a college director of admissions. And as we noted, the National Science Foundation has resisted opening the results of their review committees to public perusal and ". . . one justification offered for keeping the meetings closed was that it protects [the identity of] peer reviewers who may be 'over-zealous' in their criticisms" (Culliton, 1975b, p. 536).

We now come to the fourth undesirable condition: self-embarrassment. A secret may conceal unpopular beliefs, personal failures, errors, foibles, weaknesses, or illegal acts. A personal use of secrecy may thus shield an individual from the embarrassment (or worse) that will follow if his clandestine information or behavior becomes common knowledge. Thus a senator will let only a trusted few know the content of a bill he is preparing for presentation until it has been formally put into the senate's hopper because he fears his idea may be stolen from him (Redman, 1973). His original drafting of legislation, as a result, is done under strict precautions. Inventors are equally as careful about their creative ideas, as are informers about their true identity.

We need to remind ourselves that some people are more secretive by nature and habit than others. It is easier to avoid answering questions about a message, explaining things over and over, or accounting for a given behavior. We can therefore suppose that lazy people are more secretive than energetic persons. And it seems reasonable that persons who place great value on the status quo and who wish to avoid change are more likely to be passive and withdrawn and thus secretive as a way of keeping matters in a steady state. An example of such a person is the chairman of the board of directors of a pharmaceutical firm. He would not allow the stockholders at their meeting to advance topics that might arouse questions about a need for change in the company's ethics. Administrators with an authoritarian bent, moreover, are commonly involved in suppressing open communication to prevent social support for social change. How then do they encourage change when it is needed? Are they still secretive? Employees in a hierarchy are known to be more secretive in their contacts with superiors if they are threatened by those superiors (Cartwright and Zander, 1968a). Paranoid persons conceal their actions, and healthy people become reclusive when they are highly anxious. Individuals who are subject to punishment if they do not act as group members tell them to cover up personal misbehavior; and people who might obtain a reward only if they act in appropriate ways will conceal a failure so that they might qualify for a gain (French and Raven, 1959). All in all, as a result of personal disposition, social situation, or both, some people play their cards very close to their chests—they will go to great lengths to avoid self-embarrassment.

We just saw that secrecy is a preventive against four undesirable conditions and so is used when it can provide such protection. Under certain circumstances, like those mentioned in the following hypotheses, we expect members to devote greater efforts in behalf of secrecy.

Hypothesis: The greater the number of undesirable conditions prevented by secrecy, the more a member is willing to keep the secret.

A member may perceive there is a high probability that unwanted conditions will develop in the group if certain information becomes known there. The hypothesis proposes that the tendency to keep a secret will be stronger as the unfavorable consequences from leaking it will be greater. The undesirable conditions may affect only one part of the organization or several parts. It is conceivable, moreover, that some individuals, because of their positions in the organization, may be better able to generate undesirable conditions or to escalate them from minor ones to important ones. When this is the case, it is wise to keep the secret from such strong reactors.

Hypothesis: The more important the undesirable conditions prevented by a secret, the more a member is willing to keep the secret.

An important undesirable condition, in contrast to a minor one, creates more unwanted change in more parts of an organization for a longer period of time.

Hypothesis: A member of a group will make more effort to

keep specific information secret if he believes that his actions are an essential part of a secrecy effort.

This hypothesis holds that an individual will be more involved in secrecy if he thinks his part is essential for preventing undesirable conditions. To believe this, it is probably necessary that he understand how his failure to keep the secret could cause unwanted results, that he is in a position to keep the secret, that he is capable of keeping the secret, and that he is an important link in doing so.

Hypothesis: A number of individuals are more likely to keep a secret if they have jointly agreed that it is necessary to do so.

Anyone who discloses a secret will of course be unpopular among persons who are disadvantaged by the disclosure. This unpopularity will be more certain and stronger if the secret is a joint pledge taken by a set of persons, all of whom would suffer from its leakage. Joint promises make each participant aware that the secret is needed for common protection.

Effects of Secrecy

Secrecy is required in some settings; there is no choice in the matter. An individual may belong to an occupation, an agency, or a fraternal order that customarily expects members to keep special facts to themselves, resisting all pressures to give out this information, even if it is sought by the court. Also, those who have certain professional roles are expected to be discreet: counselors, lawyers, physicians, realtors, judges, priests, social surveyors, ambassadors, and news reporters.

In a business place, a fiduciary relationship may develop between an employee and his firm, a relationship which requires him to keep a secret for the organization if he knows, and agrees, that the company expects such discretion. This special relationship, largely based on loyalty to the group, ordinarily is effective and helps members to keep secrets more than they break them, provided the holder of the secret is not in a position that arouses his selfish motives to an excessive degree. Based on prior research

(Zander, 1971), this fiduciary relationship is stronger if the group is successful, the member is competent, and the cohesiveness of the group is strong. But secrecy can be risky for the keeper because its consequences may turn out to be different from what was intended. Thus:

Assumption: Secrecy may have effects upon an organization that are less desirable than the effects the secrecy was initially supposed to control.

Secrecy is based in the long run upon disrespect for, fear of, or sympathy for the reactions of others. Those who keep a secret are attempting to control colleagues by preventing them from knowing something that may be important to them. In a sense then, one who keeps a secret from others does not trust the reactions of "those people," and her secrecy is to some degree an expression of derogation toward them (Keller and Brown, 1974). Persons who are uninformed sense the attitudes of a secretive colleague and they, naturally enough, suspect her to be engaged in actions that cannot stand the light of day. Secrecy, therefore, often stimulates suspicion and distrust on both sides. It also may provide power for the secret keeper because it keeps others dependent on her.

The uninformed persons are even more displeased if they need the hidden information to perform their job or to change adverse circumstances within the organization. And if they feel the withheld information is *tremendously* important to them, the excluded persons will develop a negative reaction toward those who maintain secrecy. And being barred from the facts, it is reasonable to expect, may be a source of dissatisfaction and collective protest. A secret often is a valuable commodity—one can offer to trade it for some good. "I have a secret" is said with a smile, and its revelation can be a reward; those who do not learn the secret feel deprived or rejected.

A participant in clandestine behavior can easily prevent those who are not in on the secret from distrusting him by making sure that his concealment technique is leakproof and that his secreting itself is not visible. Ideally his secrecy will not generate unwanted reactions because uninformed others will have no stimulus to which they can respond. We have a hunch that such stonewalling is a burden and that it seldom persists very long if the deprived persons suspect there is a secret and try to uncover it.

Georgopoulos and Mann (1962) showed that poor communication within a hospital damages collaboration among staff members and makes the organization less efficient as a unit. Secrecy, because it is an ineffective form of communication, might therefore have such consequences as encouraging nonadherence to group standards because social pressures cannot function in the absence of communication; weakening the linkage between separate jobs and lines of authority; engendering a less than maximal performance among individuals who need secreted facts to do their jobs well; fostering the development of disparate and individual goals, rather than one goal shared by all; and reducing the variety of solutions available for consideration when a group faces a problem.

Secrecy is seldom a constructive or creative activity. Worse, it stalls the introduction of needed change because it prevents adequate feedback to members about the performance of their organization. Obviously, if there is inadequate evidence about how well their unit is doing, the members cannot accurately appraise the group's performance and identify its problems, and thus they will make few efforts to improve things. As is often the case, no news about an organization's outcomes is taken by its members to be good news (Ferguson and Kelley, 1964; Zander, 1971).

The absence of full feedback (for those who are not in on the secret) has a consequence beyond that of damaging a group's problem solving: It prevents the organization from setting rational goals for its regular tasks because such goals require a correct understanding of the group's scores on past trials. It also prevents the group from developing a motivation to do well because the group cannot develop such a desire unless there is good evidence about the quality of the group's prior performance and its perceived chances for future success (Zander, 1971). Feedback secrecy thus limits group-oriented motivation simply because it prevents members from knowing how their group is doing.

Other consequences of secrecy are familiar. When a scientist is constrained to be silent about certain ideas or the results of research or proposed actions, academic freedom is frustrated, and the bases of logic, science, and knowledge are eroded. When the results of research cannot be freely circulated, they cannot be reexamined, and the gradual approximation of the truth, by identifying and correcting errors, is not possible. Secrecy impedes scientific progress and allows hazards and half-baked theories to flower. Secrecy is a potent weapon of anyone who intends to manipulate others. Because secrecy is a preventer of change, it is used by those who wish to keep things as they are and who wish to limit their group's response to new situations. Secrecy prevents awareness of the need for change and restricts the quality of solutions that might be found for group problems.

In recent years social pressures against secrecy within large organizations have, apparently, caused more and more organizations to open up. Boards, executive bodies, and commissions now seem to have public meetings more than they used to (Culliton, 1975a; Holden, 1975b). The minutes of administrative meetings are being circulated more widely than they have been in the past, and special procedures have been invented to facilitate discussion among persons who might ordinarily be secretive in the presence of one another in a face-to-face conference (Delbeca and Van de Ven, 1971; Blake, Mouton, and Sloma, 1965). Many of these changes have been stimulated by the Freedom of Information Act passed in the late 1960s, by the reaction of the public to the attempts to conceal illegal practices in the White House, and by the increasing efforts of groups that wish to have a say about their own fate.

But despite the bad press secrecy receives and the adverse effects it creates for an organization, it is a regular part of collective life and does have some role in most organizations. Secrecy is especially appreciated by those who benefit from it, namely, those who want facts about themselves to be kept private. Citizens dislike the idea of secret dossiers, but they dislike even more the possibility that inaccurate data about themselves might be publicly revealed. Such fears are not new, of course; earlier they led to a number of articles and books about the invasion of individual privacy, in which it was proposed that there is an informal right (if not a legal one) for a person to maintain confidentiality about his own affairs and to have some influence upon who knows what about one's life history (Holden, 1975a). Privacy, it is plain, is praised in some settings, as secrecy seldom is.

Summary

Members keep secrets within an organization to prevent the development of adverse conditions there such as ineffectiveness of the organization, friction in interpersonal relations, public derogation of a specific individual, or discomfort for the secret keeper. Members are more willing to keep a secret when it appears that adverse conditions might be greater should the secret be revealed. Yet, secrecy may have effects on an organization that are less desirable than those it was initially supposed to prevent, because concealment of information is based on distrust, clandestine moves, and uncreative responses to a problem.

Chapter Three

Group Motivation and Performance

A friend of mine works hard on a memorandum about how to improve procedures in her office, even though she has not been asked to write the statement. A tackle on a football team tells a reporter he would rather play end because he is better suited to that position, but he will do whatever the team needs from him. And his coach praises not just the team but the "football program" so that everyone who has a part in it is approved. A friendly woman at my front door says she is working for her church and asks me to join it so I can help too. A neighbor reports for duty on a rescue squad because a nearby flood requires the squad's services. The chairperson of a social action committee wants to step down but decides not to because the work of the group is so important.

There is a common denominator among these instances: exertion of energy toward a goal. But each participant is more or less motivated by a source that is effective, widespread, works every time, takes no special training, and is well understood by people of affairs. Each individual is working for a specific group and wants to be sure that the group performs well. The group's goal is paramount.

Effective Group Goals

Members' concern for the fate of their group and their motivation to help the unit are of practical interest but seldom have been studied. Indeed, scholars view a group as merely a setting for study of individual behaviors, interpersonal interaction, or mutual influence. Occasionally researchers state that members' plans and energies are devoted to attaining a group's goals (not only the members' personal objectives), but this allegation is rarely tested, and its limitations are infrequently examined. Thus, this chapter will examine the reasons for group motivation. Let us consider this question by noting our first assumption:

Assumption: Some groups create a product that can be attributed to the unit as a whole, not to particular members.

A group's product may be a score, a report, a plan, or some other thing. Groups that develop such unitary products include sports teams, building firms, glass blowers, submarine crews, or factory committees who establish production goals for coming weeks. In contrast, there are sets of individuals who produce many separate products, each of which can be attributed to a given group member, not to the unit as a whole. Each participant gets credit for his own unique effort; the group does not.

Participants will be more likely to attribute their product to the group as a whole, rather than to individual members, when certain conditions prevail. Such conditions include the group repeating a given task periodically (instead of generating a single product and disbanding), the amount or quality of results from the joint product being visible to the members, the members developing some idea about how well the group will do in the future, and each and every member contributing to some degree to helping the group complete its work.

Assumption: Members of a group with a unitary product become more concerned about the quality of the group's performance than about the quality of their own personal performance.

There are data that support this assumption. For example, in a slipper factory that had twenty-eight assembly lines of eight or ten women each, I asked the workers on three occasions whether they placed more importance on their own or their group's success. In every one of the twenty-eight sets the members felt the group to be more important (Zander and Armstrong, 1972). In a study of the executive boards in forty-six United Funds, the members had more pride in their organization's success than in their personal efforts (Zander, Forward, and Albert, 1969). In an investigation of small groups in a brewery, the respondents were as concerned about their group's achievement as they were about their own and expressed much less concern for the company as a whole (Zander, 1971). And in a chemical company, professional men were satisfied with their own attainments but were not sure whether their personal goals were consonant with the goals of the firm. Even more instances of selfless service for an organization abound: the ill actress who joins her colleagues (instead of staying in bed) because the show must go on, the tired but persistent envelope stuffer in a local political party, and the substitute who works hard at practice even though he never plays in a game.

A distinction implicit in the second assumption is that a member has the choice of working for himself, working for his group, working for both himself and the group, or working for neither. Furthermore, these separate motives may be similar and may supplement one another, or they may be contradictory and weaken each other. Forward (1969) showed that group- and self-oriented motives are often independent. A person can work for his group without benefiting himself because group gains are more important to him than personal gains. The opposite can also occur. This useful distinction is too seldom made in studies of groups because it is assumed that persons always work in a group only to benefit themselves.

Assumption: A member who experiences satisfaction from his group's success develops a desire that his group attain additional success; one who experiences dissatisfaction from his group's failure develops a desire that his group avoid additional failure—he develops a motive for the group's achievement.

Among persons who are concerned about the group's fate, either or both of two dispositions can develop. The *desire for group success* is a disposition of a participant to experience pride in his group if it successfully accomplishes a challenging group task. The *desire to avoid group failure* is a disposition of a member to be embarrassed with his group if it fails on a challenging task. We assume these motives are not permanent traits of individuals but are the products of a particular setting at a particular time.

For members to become convinced that their group is in fact succeeding or failing, they must have experienced a number of trials in the same group task, must know what scores on that task are considered elsewhere to be poor or excellent, must agree among themselves on the score their own group should strive to attain, and must be able to see how closely each group score comes to the previously established goal. To arouse either the motive to approach group success or the motive to avoid group failure, one must accordingly provide repetitions on a unitary group task and ask members to estimate how well the group will do before each trial (Zander, 1971). In this way members become involved in attaining their group's goal.

There is as yet no reliable measure of group-oriented motives that is useful in natural settings. Thus the presence and strength of these motives have been detected through the observation of events that (it is assumed) can occur only if a group-oriented disposition exists. There also is no evidence about how long such situationally aroused dispositions last. Do they fade over time? If so, why?

Assumption: The strength of a member's desire for group success changes as conditions in the group change.

What kind of conditions might strengthen or weaken a member's desire for group success? Seven hypotheses can be suggested in regard to this issue, but only four have been studied; the rest merit investigation. For the sake of simplicity, we will not consider ways of enhancing the desire to avoid group failure.

Hypothesis: The more members are responsible for a group's fate, the stronger their desire for the group's success.

A member who knows that his group needs his efforts will want to make sure that the group's product is a source of pride to him. This assertion is based on an early finding by Pepitone (1952), who observed that individual members of a group produced more (quantity and quality) if their assignment was described to them as important to the group; they produced less if their assignment was said to be unimportant, even though all members (unknown to all) were performing exactly the same activity at the same moment. In accordance with Pepitone's observation, two more specific predictions can be made.

Hypothesis: A central member of a group, in contrast to a peripheral one, will develop a stronger desire for group success.

A central person is one who has greater responsibility for the group's product because she leads the way, sets the pace, does the most crucial set of acts, or reaches the final decision. A peripheral person does none of these things. This hypothesis was supported in two laboratory experiments and in a questionnaire study of forty-six executive committees (Zander, 1971).

Hypothesis: Members of a strong group, in contrast to members of a weak group, will have a greater desire for group success.

In one experiment, strong groups were created by seating members tightly around a table, addressing them as "this group," asking them to choose a name for their team, and so on, helping them to see themselves as a single entity. Weak groups were created by seating a set of strangers on randomly arranged chairs and addressing them as individuals ("each of you") during the study. The idea was that in a strong group, more than in a weak group, members will perceive that a group exists, that they are within rather than outside it, and that their actions will affect events in that group. The results of an experiment by Zander and Medow (1965) supported this hypothesis.

The following predictions, also pertinent to our first hypothesis, have not been tested: A member will develop a stronger desire for group success: the longer he has been a member of the group, the greater the cohesiveness of the group, the more groupmates desire the group to be successful, and the fewer the members in the group.

Hypothesis: When a group succeeds, a member's desire for group success is stronger as the group's task is more difficult. When a group fails, a member's desire to avoid group failure is stronger as the group's task is easier.

This hypothesis is based on our third assumption, that success arouses a taste for more success and failure a taste for less failure. It implies, however, that satisfaction from a success is greater when the task is harder, and repulsiveness of a failure is greater when the task is easier. This implication is discussed more fully elsewhere (Zander, 1971, pp. 54–57). The hypothesis received support in experiments by Zander and Medow (1963) and Forward (1969).

Hypothesis: A more competent member of a group, in contrast to a less competent one, develops a stronger desire for group success.

The less competent person worries about his own personal failures, and the more competent member is confident about himself and turns his energy to ensuring a group success.

Hypothesis: As observers approve of the group to a greater degree, the members' desire for group success becomes stronger. The approval by observers certifies to members that their group is succeeding—something that is not always obvious to them.

Hypothesis: As leaders of a group convince members to value pride in their group, their desire for group success becomes stronger. Members wish their group to succeed so that they can feel proud of it; the more value members place on pride, the more they desire to succeed.

Communication and the Desire for Group Success

More communication among group members leads to a stronger desire for the group's success. While the American expedition was ascending Mount Everest, Richard Emerson, one of the climbers, who is interested in team motivation and communication, made standard preplanned comments to his colleagues and recorded their answers on a small tape machine he lugged along. Emerson had predicted that the remarks team members would make to one another, while attempting the climb, would maximize their joint motivation to succeed. That is, if Emerson made a discouraging comment, the colleague's rejoinder would be a cheerful one, and if he made an optimistic comment, the respondent's remark would dampen that ardor. Both kinds of responses would foster a moderately challenging goal and thus would be maximally motivating. The actual comments by his teammates were as Emerson had expected they would be (Emerson, 1966). It appears, therefore, that through interpersonal communication members may fashion a commonly shared desire for group success. In a few investigations in the laboratory I studied the effect of communication among team members and noticed these (as yet unpublished) results:

1. After they finished working on a group test, members privately completed individual brief questionnaires that measured their feelings about their team and the work it had done. Following that, the members had a group discussion in which they were to reach a unanimous decision on the same matters. During the discussions the participants became more approaching if that had been their inclination before the discussion began and more avoiding if that had been their preference. Thus, discussion strengthened members' private dispositions.

2. In another experiment, members working on a group assignment that required close integration of their movements were

allowed to talk freely in one condition and were denied any opportunity to talk in a contrasting condition. The groups in which participants were allowed to talk set more challenging goals than those in which participants were not allowed to talk. Thus mere chatter apparently invoked a stronger desire for group success.

3. Communication is more frequent among members when there is a division of labor than when there is not (Zander and Wolfe, 1964), in a cooperative group than in a competitive one (Deutsch, 1949), and in a group with a harder task than in one with an easier task (Zander and Ledvinka, in Zander, 1971).

4. Finally, in a field study of many districts in an insurance company, members' emphasis on achieving group goals was greater when a manager encouraged more face-to-face interaction among the members of his staff. Productivity and satisfaction with the job was better, moreover, as the members placed more emphasis on goal achievement (Bowers and Seashore, 1966).

Assumption: As the strength of members' desire for group success increases, their efforts to achieve group success increase.

When members have a stronger desire for group success, naturally they are expected to do things that arouse pride in their group, either through improving its performance or through modifying its criterion of success. Many moves are available to members toward such an end; these moves are presented as the following five hypotheses.

Hypothesis: The stronger the members' desire for group success, the more they will choose a moderately challenging goal rather than an easy or a difficult one.

A moderately challenging goal is a bit more difficult than the group's best level of performance. Members who seek pride in their group's success will not want an easy group goal because its attainment will provide little satisfaction, and they will not want a hard goal because that might be failed and provide little satisfaction. Thus they choose a goal level that best balances the chances of obtaining a satisfactory success and avoiding a repulsive failure. Findings that support this hypothesis were reported in Zander (1971). There is evidence which suggests that members with a stronger desire for group success are more able to resist social pressures toward irrational goals.

Hypothesis: The stronger the members' desire to avoid group failure, the more they choose a goal that is other than a moderate challenge.

In this prediction it is assumed that the members of a failing group prefer either a very easy goal because that will prevent the likelihood of further failure or a very hard goal because that will provide little dissatisfaction if the goal is not attained. Either goal, easy or hard, lets the members avoid any shame or embarrassment that might accompany a failure by the group. Investigations indicating the reasonableness of this hypothesis are described in Zander (1971).

Hypothesis: The stronger the members' desire for group success, the more their comments reveal a desire to work on the group's task.

Members prove they want to succeed on their joint task by encouraging, praising, or suggesting ways of improving procedures; they prove they want to avoid failure by blaming one another, criticizing aspects of the task, or proposing that they all take it easy. Avoiding remarks are expected to occur more often if members have a stronger desire to avoid the consequences of failure.

An experiment to test this hypothesis was not successful because members made more approaching comments than avoiding ones, regardless of the motive that supposedly had been aroused in them by the experimenter and regardless of the success or failure of the group. Perhaps the desire to avoid group failure does not last very long when the task is a challenging one because that desire is soon replaced by the desire to attain group success. Or, it might be considered better form to keep encouraging one another, even when a group is failing.

Hypothesis: The stronger the members' desire for group success, the more their motivated beliefs reveal a tendency to work hard on the group's job.

Motivated beliefs are members' views which reveal that they are satisfied by and prepared to engage in work for the group, or dissatisfied by and ready to avoid such participation. Examples of approaching beliefs are when members describe themselves as interested in the group's activity, say they are eager to do well, anticipate effort from colleagues, state it is important to do better than other teams, or expect colleagues to be helpful to one another. Examples of avoiding beliefs are revealed by unfavorable responses to such matters as personal responsibility for the group's score, personal part in the group's work, helpfulness attributed to groupmates, reliability of the group's score as a measure of its ability, or willingness to abandon the practice of setting goals for the group. This hypothesis was validated in results reported in Zander (1971).

Hypothesis: The stronger the members' desire for group success, the better the group performs.

During tests of this hypothesis in the laboratory, performance was measured on group tasks that required the use of muscular energy, speed of motor movement, persistence on a task, accuracy in counting objects, and amount of oral chatter. Outside the laboratory, performance was measured by number of sales, speed in hiking through snow during a period of four days, and production on assembly lines. In all of these instances the hypothesis was generally supported (Zander, 1971).

The effect of stronger desire for group success ought to be evident in other ways, as in the following hypotheses, none of which have been tested.

Hypotheses: Members with greater desire for group success: will want more information about their group's performance so they can accurately judge the chances of future success; will want more information about the scores other groups are attaining; will compete more ardently against rival groups; will more closely fit their own goals to those of their group; or will pay more attention to their group's experience than to their own personal performance.

Summary

Members of a group may have, or may develop, a motivation concerned with the achievement of their group as a unit. This group motivation is more likely to develop if the group creates a product that can be attributed to the effort of the unit as a whole, not just to particular members. Persons within such a working group become more concerned about the quality of the group's performance than about the quality of their own personal performance and develop a desire for group success. The members' desire for group success becomes stronger if, for example, the group is a stronger unit, the participants have a more central role in the work of the group, and the group has been successful in the past. When members have a greater desire for group success they do things that will result in pride in the group; as a consequence, members with a stronger desire for group success work to develop qualities in the group that are usually valued there.

Chapter Four

Choosing Difficult Goals

For a number of years I have saved every printed story I find that describes the creation of a new group because I am interested in the varied purposes of groups. I have noticed that such purposes are given prime attention in a group's birth announcement (but only briefly and vaguely noted in accounts of established groups).

New groups are unreasonably optimistic about their futures; that is, their objectives are very difficult, but the paths to these goals seem fairly easy at first. For example, some students want to establish a new scientific journal or start a third national political party.

Or some citizens want to improve the ethics of the pharmaceutical industry or band together to eliminate crime. These objectives do not seem difficult, but they really are because the groups do not consider, for example, their lack of funds, need for more members, inadequate talent, or absent social support. All each group has is a purpose, a respect for that purpose, and a willingness to meet and talk about it; mundane tasks such as deciding on the structure of the organization, assigning jobs to members, designating officers, and so on supposedly will take care of themselves.

This glowing optimism may be caused by the inexperience of the group's spokesmen, the group's desire for the approval they will get if they meet difficult goals, or the vagueness of groups' plans when goals are not clearly thought through. Most empirical investigations into group goals have concentrated on units that repeat the same task a number of times and set a goal before each new trial, after learning how well they did on the previous task. Thus, the groups are engaged in a feedback cycle. These repetitious cycles enable researchers to investigate why one particular goal was selected rather than another and whether a different goal was chosen later based on specific past experience. Often, in this type of research a group is wholly free to make its own choices with no external influences acting on it. In other cases, external agents press the group to perform at a specific level, and the members' acceptance or rejection of the external pressures becomes a focus of research. In still other instances, the group is part of a larger system, such as the executive board of a business organization, enabling researchers in both the laboratory and in natural settings to examine how a smaller unit affects a larger institution. As a result of empirical investigations we can state our first assumption:

Assumption: A group that is working toward a set of explicit goals seems to prefer more difficult goals to goals that are easy.

Before we ask why groups lean toward hard goals, let us discuss the evidence that supports this assumption. Groups that repeatedly perform the same task fall short of their goals more often than they reach them, which means that the group selected goals that were too difficult. In many financial campaigns, for instance, there are more failures than successes because goals are set too high (Zander, Forward, and Albert, 1969), and in a slipper factory with numerous assembly lines, only two or three of the lines achieved the goals that the members were allowed to select for their own group (Zander and Armstrong, 1972).

In the laboratory, where group members are asked to change their goal between trials whenever they believe this change is necessary, the members more often move the goal upward after a success than downward after a failure (Zander, 1971). If the members do not know whether their group has succeeded or failed on a given trial, they raise their group's goal for the next trial and seldom lower it (Zander, 1971). The officials of failing United Fund organizations infrequently lower their goals, whereas those in succeeding Funds raise their goals after each success. And there is this same upward tendency in goal setting among managers who set goals for subordinates. When superiors press teams, members are quite unwilling to lower their goals, even after a failure. As a result, the team's goals eventually become too hard to accomplish (Zander and Armstrong, 1972).

The amount of discrepancy between a group's past score and a goal it chooses for a future attempt is larger after a failure than after a success. Over a series of trials, therefore, failing groups, compared to succeeding ones, develop a larger discrepancy between past levels of performance and levels of future goals (Zander, 1971).

Reasons for Choosing Difficult Goals

The evidence just presented raises many questions, including the most obvious one of why a group would select, and keep selecting, hard goals. We shall attempt to explain these events in the following three assumptions, then we shall consider how a group may be persuaded to choose a goal that is not too difficult.

Assumption: Members prefer a group goal that is likely to be attained and will provide satisfaction from its attainment.

As group members learn the results of their repeated trials, they begin to sense what level of accomplishment their group is able (and not able) to attain. When thinking about what their group might achieve in the future, therefore, experienced members are ready to estimate what score their group can reasonably strive for. Naturally, they will perceive less chance of reaching a harder level than an easier one. But the group will most often select a more difficult goal because the amount of *satisfaction* members anticipate they will receive if they accomplish a specific goal will be *greater* if that goal is difficult than if it is easy, and the amount of *dissatisfaction* if the group fails to reach its goal will be *less* if the goal is difficult than if it is easy. In other words, the participants know they will feel better after meeting a harder challenge than failing a simpler one, or, if they fail a difficult task, they will feel that at least they tried—the ultimate consequences of *either* a success or a failure are better while striving to meet a hard rather than an easy goal.

Thus group members select the goal that best resolves any conflict between the attractiveness of success, the repulsiveness of failure, and the estimated chances of success or failure. The group sets their goal at a level that will provide as much satisfaction or as little dissatisfaction for them as possible. In view of this, we can see why a goal is raised more often after a success than lowered after a failure: There is more likelihood of dissatisfaction in the future from lowering a goal than there is from keeping it at the same level it was in the past or even raising it a bit. If a group lowers its goals, they will feel that they took the easy way out. But by keeping difficult goals, or trying to attain even harder goals, a group will satisfy itself that they are doing their best, and if they keep achieving these hard (or harder) goals, they will continue to derive satisfaction.

Assumption: The stronger the members' desire for the group's success, the more members prefer a goal that will provide favorable consequences.

When a person is a member of a group with a given mission, she usually becomes interested in the unit's level of achievement. This is contrary to most research on group goals, which assumes that group objectives are an indirect product of a joint agreement among self-centered individuals who reach some sort of compromise about mutual and personal goals. Actually, when one observes a group while it is making a decision, one notes that members often suppress any inclination to put their own needs first and pay little attention to individual's desires, behaving instead in a way which is primarily for the good of the group. Understandably, then, members' motives to achieve success may be based not only on obtaining personal rewards but on attaining satisfactory outcomes (rather than embarrassing failures) for the group as a whole (Zander and Ulberg, 1971).

As observed in Chapter Three the strength of a member's desire for group success is different in different situations. Generally, it appears to be stronger among individuals who have a greater commitment to their group. Because participants who have a stronger desire for group success want to benefit from the favorable consequences of their group's effort, and because these consequences are more relevant to the group than to the individual person, a member with a stronger desire for group success should favor the group goal that is most likely to provide favorable consequences for that group. She will want her group to have a challenging goal (a goal a bit harder than the group has achieved up to that point) because the chances of developing pride in the group are greater when a group meets a hard goal than when it meets an easy task. And as the desire for group success becomes stronger within a group and as the group's successes accumulate, the difficulty level of future goals will steadily rise (Zander and Ulberg, 1971).

Also, we can suppose that the strength of members' desires to avoid group failure becomes greater if they feel less responsible for their group's fate (they have peripheral roles or are newcomers), belong to weaker groups, have a stronger personal motive to avoid the effects of individual failure, or are less attracted to their membership in that group, and therefore are not very troubled if the group experiences the unfavorable consequences of group failure. The goal choices of members who fear group failure may be erratic, neither consistently harder nor easier, but in most cases these people apparently choose too difficult goals to get credit for aiming high even though their group fails to reach their impossible objective. Unfortunately such notions have been seldom studied.

Assumption: External pressures on a group to choose a given goal are more likely to be directed toward a difficult goal than toward an easy one.

Pressures on a group to work toward a particular goal arise from four sources: (1) a request for help by dependent persons outside the group, (2) a set of scores obtained by other comparable groups, (3) comments made about the group by people in a position to see the group at work, or (4) a direct order from an individual who has the right to make such a demand. Each source of pressure may affect the level of a group's goals under particular conditions, as we will see in the following explanations.

A group's goal is not really a matter of choice if there is a request from outsiders. For example, if a special manufacturing department receives some unusual orders, the sales personnel (and the customers) get what they want from the company's workers, even if fulfilling the unusual orders involves considerable effort on the part of the workers. The exotic order has to be filled because it is a legitimate request, a part of the understanding between the sales force and the assembly unit: The sales people have the right to promise delivery of a new and different need, and the assemblers' duty is to meet the schedule.

As another example, each year budget committees of the United Fund receive requests from local welfare agencies. These requests are considered when the committees set their upcoming fiscal goals. Not surprisingly, the committee members are aware that the monetary requests by welfare agencies increase in dollar amounts each year, which means the United Fund has to set higher and higher goals. Thus, when asked why their campaign goals were often unreasonably high, United Fund members said that since welfare agencies require yearly increases in their budgets, lowering the financial goals might make it necessary for the agencies to leave the United Fund in order to solicit their own funds independently and thus the fund would not fulfill the needs of the community. And it is important that the fund does fulfill community needs: Several hundred fund members replied in a survey that helping the United Fund meet the needs of welfare agencies gave them the most job satisfaction (Zander, Forward, and Albert, 1969).

These two examples illustrate that people who depend on a goal-setting group can influence the level of that group's goals. And the needs of the external agents often become harder rather than easier, thus leading to more difficult goals for the helping group. Unfortunately, no studies have been conducted on what conditions cause a group to refuse help dependent others and refuse to change its goals when asked to do so.

The second external pressure that influences a group to select a difficult goal is social comparison. Groups often exist in multiples, such as assembly lines in a factory, departmental faculties in a college, platoons in an army, or basketball teams in a gym. When the "score" of each group is available to all similar groups, each group compares its record with that of the others. As a result of such social comparisons, a group may decide to modify its goals.

An example of the effects caused by social comparison was obtained from a controlled laboratory study of many teams working on a motor task. After each of fourteen trials, half the groups were told the average score of all the other groups, and half the groups were given no such information. The reported averages were fixed so it seemed that a given team was either doing much better than the other teams or much worse. Regardless of the scores their group had actually earned, those who could see that their unit was worse than the average group set high goals, and those who could see that their group was better than the average group set low goals. Thereafter the newly chosen higher goals remained fixed, but the lower goals were soon abandoned—members raised their goals to match the ones typically chosen after a modest success, even though these goals were too difficult. Apparently the effect of doing worse than other groups was more influential in determining goal choices than the effect of besting other groups (Zander and Medow, 1965).

The national association that establishes professional standards for United Funds encourages each community to compare the quality of its own campaign with the quality of the campaigns in five or so other communities. The association provides a cookbook of procedures for trustees of a local fund to follow in deciding which towns they will use as models for these social comparisons. Although I have seen no data on the effects of such city by city comparisons, my guess is that the funds prefer to compare their own town with ones similar in size and economy and will select goals more difficult than any these towns have reached. Studies of the effects of intergroup comparisons upon group goal setting are needed.

Now we come to the third external pressure on a group: evaluative comments about the group by outside observers. Observers are persons who do not belong to the group and who have no authority to, or need to, put direct pressure on the unit. Because these observers have informed themselves about the quality of the group's work, and have made evaluative appraisals of it, their remarks will be of much interest to members.

In a laboratory study, a group working on an activity that required close teamwork was watched by observers who were seated behind a glass screen. Before each trial the observers discussed and decided what score they believed the performing team would be able to earn on its next trial, and this prediction was delivered to the working group. When the observers expected the group would do well on its next attempt, the predictions had a stronger effect on the goals of the group (the goals were set higher) than when the observers predicted the group would do poorly (goals were kept the same—not changed). Thus, in this case, external expectations pressing toward harder goals seemed to be more influential than ones pressing toward easier goals (Zander, 1971). But surely that cannot always be so, as will be seen in other studies of social pressures described later.

The fourth external pressure on a group is a direct order from an individual. The most familiar example of this type of pressure is a superior ordering a group to reach a given level of attainment. This order may be accompanied by an offer of a reward if the group does as it is told or by a punishment if it does not. Such a superior ordinarily wants a good score rather than a poor one from the group. As a case in point, in the slipper factory, managers set daily goals for each assembly line. These goals were not reached 80 percent of the days, yet the managers lowered the goals only 20 percent of the days. The managers explained that their repeated announcements of the goals were based on a need for sufficient productivity to ensure a profit and on a belief, supported by time and motion studies, that each group, if it tried, could do as well as it was being asked to do (Zander and Armstrong, 1972).

The managers believed that the goals they set for each unit were not strict demands because no team was required to fulfill the goals set for it, and there were no rewards or punishments for the employees if they did or did not attain the goals—workers were paid just an annual salary, with no bonuses or commissions. The proffered goals were, in a sense, merely standards of excellence.

Because group members appear to have a predilection for harder goals, it is not surprising that social pressure on a group to choose a difficult level is more effective than pressure on it to choose an easier level. But requests for better performance typically generate more failures than successes, yet the group's aspiration is not always lowered after the failure. And pressures toward a lower output generate more successes than failure, so the goal is usually raised after a success. To some unknown degree, then, a charge given to a group to set a more difficult standard may be more influential (or appear to be so) in determining a group's goal because members ordinarily dislike lowering their aspiration after a failure, and a charge to set an easier goal may be less influential (or appear to be so) because members prefer raising their group's goal after a success. It seems probable that members' responses to their group's success or failure and their responses to external social pressures each affect the other in such a way that the contribution of one may be simply a product of the other. We need therefore to examine separately the effect of external pressures and the effect of success and failure, as was done in a laboratory experiment.

The study was so constructed that every group failed on part of the trials and succeeded on part of the trials in attaining goals set by the team members. Immediately after half of each of the failing trials, members were asked to raise their goal, and after the other half of the failures a request to lower it. After half of the successes, the members were likewise asked to raise their goal, and after the other half a request to lower it. It was expected that the request to set a harder goal would be more effective than the request to set an easier goal. That happened, but only because pressures directed toward an easier goal were rejected when the group had just been successful in attaining its goal and thus would regularly prefer raising its goal, rather than lowering it. When adjustments were made (statistically) for the natural tendency of members to prefer harder goals, one could see that external pressure on a group to select a difficult goal was apparently no more influential than pressure on it to choose an easy goal. The pressure on the group, moreover, was more influential in determining the level of the group's goal when it was in the direction members already intended to move the goal—toward a higher level after a success and a lower level after a failure. When the pressure upon the group was in a direction that opposed their tendency to shift the goals, the members more readily listened to the views put forth by one another of their colleagues and then set their group's goal based on their group's past performance rather than on the basis of demands from outsiders (Zander and Ulberg, 1971).

We have considered the impact of several kinds of stimuli that arise outside the boundaries of a group. Is one generally more effective than the other? There is no clear indication of this. In an experiment that compared the three forms of social pressure—the effects of meeting others' needs, of social comparison, and of overt demands on a group—each pressure had a wholly independent effect, about equal in size. The stronger each condition, the more impact it had on the group's goals. Thus members appear to have no persistent tendency to respond more readily to one form of social pressure than to another, all else being equal. It appears that what matters is whether the direction of the demand makes sense to members and is acceptable on those grounds (Forward and Zander, 1971).

Choosing a Group Goal That Is Not Too Difficult

We observed that three conditions may have a part in determining the group goal members choose: (1) the attractiveness of a given level of difficulty, (2) the desire for group success, and (3) the external pressure acting on the group. (Other sources of influence on group goals also merit study, such as the value placed on achievement in separate cultures; how members explain their group's performance; the amount of pride or shame aroused by this explanation; and how changes in equipment, management, skill of members, or whatever affect the participants' control over their group's performance.) Each of the three goal-influencing explanations is potent in its own right, and each disposes members in its own way toward favoring hard rather than easy goals. Because each explanation is independent of the other two, it is worth noting that these separate conditions can exist simultaneously in a group and that each can add its separate impact on determining the goal which is chosen.

Thus it would be useful to help a group choose a challenging goal rather than a very difficult one because a challenging goal generates a better performance, greater likelihood of future success, and more beliefs among members that are conducive to effective operation of the group. Here are seven things a leader or member can do to ensure that a group selects a challenging goal rather than an unreasonably hard or easy one.

1. Obtain an accurate measure of the group's performance and give this information to members after each performance. The need for such feedback has been implied rather than made explicit here, but it is necessary if a goal is to be chosen rationally; members cannot take their group's past output into account unless they know what it is. And past scores provide the potential basis for a standard of excellence against which a group can compete in the future with satisfaction. Without evidence about past scores, groups tend to select unwise goals.
2. Foster a desire among members to value the consequences of success. This desire can be aroused by pointing out the favorable consequences of a good performance by the group and emphasizing the importance of these consequences. The exact nature of

such consequences differ from group to group, but generally they have to do with the pride of members in their unit and the approval the group obtains after a success.

3. Increase the strength of the desire to achieve success. The strength can be enhanced by convincing members that each has an important role in the work of the group; that each depends on the others for the success of the unit; that the group is strong, attractive, and successful; and that colleagues believe in the importance of pride in their group.
4. Play down the fear of what can happen if the group fails. The desire to avoid group failure can be reduced by strengthening the desire for group success and by stressing the significance of seeking pride in the group rather than avoiding shame. Fear of failure causes members to avoid work on the task, to lose interest in obtaining the group's goal, to lose interest in the group itself, to become irresponsible in selecting a group goal, and to be embarrassed when the group fails. It does not necessarily cause a group to get a worse score.
5. Encourage members to compare the performance of their group with groups similar to their own. Comparisons between one's own group and a closely similar group are taken seriously and are unlikely to suggest unreasonable objectives.
6. Place reasonable demands on the group, not unreasonable ones. Demonstrate that a small rise in the level of goal is more motivating than a large rise.
7. Support changes within the group that will make it possible for members to work effectively in behalf of their team. These changes might be in improving the skills of members, the equipment available to them, the organization among them, or the management of the group.

If these ideas and results of research are supported in future studies and practical experience, it is plain that a wise manager should view an impossible group goal as both a cause and a result of unwanted group characteristics. A modestly difficult goal will be seen, on the other hand, as a source and consequence of desirable qualities in a group.

Summary

A group sets difficult goals more often than it sets easy ones. Three explanations for this phenomenon are notable. First, members prefer a group goal that is likely to be attained, on the one hand, and provides greater satisfaction from attaining it, on the other. Second, the more members desire group success, the more they prefer a goal that will provide favorable consequences. Third, external pressures on a group to choose a given goal are more likely to be directed toward a difficult goal than toward an easy one. Because reasonably challenging goals are more beneficial for a group than goals that are unduly hard or very easy, members will be wise to ensure that a group selects a challenging goal.

Chapter Five

Group Embarrassment

When a group is doing poorly on a task that will not be finished for some time, we expect the members to do whatever they can to improve its effectiveness. We may observe instead that they put their effort into overcoming embarrassment caused by the group's bad performance and do little to improve the group. Consider these five examples. In a slipper factory, the least productive assembly lines do not try to increase their productivity; instead, they conceal their low scores from other teams. A group of salespeople is told that their profit is worse than the profit of other groups. During staff meetings the salespeople assert that they are not in fact performing poorly and do not need to improve at all; because the company is improperly using profit as its criterion of success. Effort is what should count. The American Medical Association (AMA) creates a drug council to advise doctors on the best uses of medicines. Pharmaceutical firms, the heaviest advertisers in the association's journals, complain about the council's evaluations of their products and threaten to stop advertising in AMA publications. To forestall such threats, the AMA abolishes the drug council and provides no more advice to doctors about medicines (Dowling, 1973). A local United Fund fails to achieve its goal in a series of financial campaigns. Instead of lowering the goal to a more attainable level, the executive secretary and members of the board take things into their own hands and appeal directly to community leaders, bypassing the volunteers who are responsible for soliciting these contributions. The fund fails again. An engineering research unit fails in an attempt to hire any women and minority members; this failure becomes publicly known. Even though few such persons have been trained in that field, the unit is determined to hire enough of these individuals to constitute 25 percent of its personnel in the next two years—a very difficult goal that will not be a source of shame if it is failed.

Reducing Embarrassment

Why might an emphasis on reducing embarrassment occur? We can approach an explanation through four simple assumptions about how members cope with failure by their group.

Assumption: Members' reactions to their group's failure may have one of two emphases: planning how the group may be successful in the future or reducing embarrassment caused by the group's poor performance.

Planning ways of achieving success requires that members concentrate on problems in their unit. To do this the members may lower their criteria of group success so that these goals are more attainable. Or, they try to improve the group's procedures, equipment, tools, supplies, or skills. Attempting to reduce embarrassment requires participants to make efforts that help them duck the impact of a poor group score, change its meaning, distort its nature, or do other things which reduce the shame they feel.

Assumption: After a series of failures by a group, members will place more weight on reducing their embarrassment than on ensuring future success because there is a better chance (given the group's recent failure) of lowering embarrassment than of attaining success.

When a group's scores have been bad enough for long enough, the members become more interested in abolishing feelings of shame than in attaining feelings of pride. There is no empirical support for this proposition, but we need such an assumption to account for the members' greater emphasis on avoiding shame than on seeking pride. It is not clear how much a group must fail before members decide they have endured enough—that issue warrants investigation. Nor is it clear why members will choose one means rather than another in attempting to lower their group-relevant shame. The following notions will be more useful when that issue is resolved.

Our interest is limited to groups with special qualities: They have a specific task, they repeat it periodically, their members regularly learn the group's "score" after each trial, their members have a standard of excellence for their group's score, and their members have some influence on their group's goal for each new trial. Although we do not know which actions members initiate most often to reduce the embarrassment caused by a poor group performance, we know how members feel about their group's output in such situations and what they want to do about these feelings, based on answers to questionnaires in field and laboratory research (Zander, 1971). We shall treat those responses as though they are the actions members actually would employ were they able and allowed to do so. Embarrassment-reducing responses might concentrate, we expect, on one or more of the following aspects of group life: (1) the group's goal, (2) the group's way of doing its work, or (3) the member's own responsibility to the group.

When the group's goal is the focus, members seek to convince themselves, or others, that the group is being improperly held to a given standard of excellence. They can do this in several ways, as illustrated by the following four hypotheses.

Hypothesis: The more a group has failed, the more the members prefer an impossibly difficult goal.

As a rule, a group will lower its goal after a failure and raise it after a success. But not uncommonly a group fails, and members make no attempt to lower its aim; they may instead raise it to a more difficult level. Merely working toward a harder goal does not in itself control the members' embarrassment. But if the group fails, their embarrassment will be less if their goal has been a hard one than if it has been an easy one (Zander, 1971). In fact, some organizations seem deliberately to select unreasonably difficult objectives so the members need not be ashamed of a failure; they instead may be proud of attempting to attain an impossible end. Also, the group may be praised by nonmembers for attempting to reach this difficult objective.

Hypothesis: The more a group has failed, the more members say that attaining the goal is not worth the effort.

Some findings indicate that this hypothesis is credible. On the executive boards of United Funds, for example, members from failing funds were more likely to say, compared to those from successful funds, that it had not been important to achieve the goal their fund had failed (Zander, Forward, and Albert, 1969). In the laboratory, members of failing teams, in contrast to those on successful teams, regularly said there was little benefit from doing well on the group's task (Zander, 1971). Members sometimes refuse to set a goal for their group at all because if there is no goal there can be no failure. Or they may participate in selecting and agreeing on a goal for their group but privately hold a different goal for themselves, an action that amounts to rejection of the group's goal (Zander and Curtis, 1965). Among all United Funds, some each year wish to be excused from setting any goal, saying they prefer to do the best they can or to do a bit better than last time.

A different means for deflating the importance of failure is for a group to change the content of its goal. In a mirror factory, workers on small assembly lines were allowed to choose a goal for their unit's productivity in the hope that this would help these teams increase their output. After some experience in setting their group's goals, the workers suggested that they set goals for the costs they generate rather than for the production they turn out because cost reductions were more readily under their control and thus more attainable. Thereafter, the workers set goals for reducing scrap loss, errors, and amount of material used, but goals for productivity were no longer chosen by the members.

Hypothesis: The more a group has failed, the more members are inclined to see the external demands on the group to be easier than they in fact are.

Persons outside a group often press it to attain a given goal. When this pressure is successful, and the group fails to attain that goal, members may reduce their chagrin by telling themselves that the goal presented by the outsiders was really lower than their group's score, even though it was not (Zander and Curtis, 1965). Or members may decide to favor their own goal in preference to the one laid on them by outsiders, making their chosen goal easier than the one asked of the group (Zander and Ulberg, 1971).

Hypothesis: The more a group has failed, the more members deny that they are embarrassed by its failures.

A simple way to avoid embarrassment is to deny that it exists. The members assume that "you win some and you lose some." Shame over failure is to be expected, and to be forgotten. Sports teams often use this form of rationalization, especially those teams at the bottom of the standings.

Hypothesis: The more a group has failed, the more members blame the procedures used in doing the group's work.

In a laboratory experiment, oral comments among members were recorded while the subjects worked on a joint task. When a group failed on a given trial, most of the members' comments were derogatory about their way of collaborating and the ineptness of the members during that attempt. When it succeeded, the remarks were favorable about one another's skill and the methods the group employed (Zander, Fuller, and Armstrong, 1972).

A group's methods can be blamed in other ways. One approach is to derogate how its output is measured. Members may doubt that the group's score is correct, that the task is a true test of the group's ability (they can do better on other things), or that observers' ratings of their group are valid.

Hypothesis: The more a group has failed, the more members misrecall the group's score.

Members may remember, after their group has failed, that their group's productivity was greater than it was in fact. Such distortions have often been noticed in both natural and laboratory settings.

Finally, when a group fails, members may be ashamed of their personal output. We assume such feelings occur because a member gives a lower evaluation to his personal contribution if his group earns a poorer evaluation. A feasible way for a member to avoid this low regard of himself is to seek some means for reducing his responsibility for the group's poor outcome. The member makes no effort to change his group-oriented feelings; he instead concentrates on reducing shame over his own poor showing.

Hypothesis: The more a group has failed, the more individual members deny they were at fault.

Any participant may believe that others, not she, are to blame for the group's poor work and the group's low score therefore is not a valid indicator of her own personal worth. One who has a less responsible role in a group should be more ready to blame her colleagues (not herself) than one who has a more responsible role and knows that she must be at fault in some degree. Thus, a member in a failing group may tell herself that she has a minor position and that blame for the group's weak production cannot be put on her because her contribution is so small. Or she may do little for her group so that she can see herself as having only a small part in the group's output. She may even leave the unit to avoid shame by association. It is often observed that failing groups lose members rapidly and find it hard to recruit new ones (Cartwright, 1968; Blanchard, Adelman, and Cook, 1975).

Perhaps a member will not be ashamed of herself after her group fails if her own assignment was too much for her. Also, if she has put out considerable effort for the group, she may be less embarrassed after a group's failure. But if she knows she is competent and is aware she has put out little effort for the group, she is likely to be personally humiliated by her group's failure (Zander, Fuller, and Armstrong, 1972).

Assumption: Actions taken to reduce group-oriented embarrassment do little toward ensuring a future success; thus a group that focuses on lowering embarrassment will most likely fail again.

A circular causal system may develop in the coping behaviors of members, not unlike the cycle of behavior in a neurotic individual. The three steps in the cycle are: (1) a group's obvious failures arouse an attempt to reduce the embarrassment members feel; (2) a form of coping that does not improve productivity is used, and thus failure occurs again; (3) this new failure once more generates efforts to reduce embarrassment, leading to another failure. In contrast, a success stimulates opposite conditions in all respects and thus leads to future successes. Examples of these circular-causal cycles in groups were observed by Zander, Forward, and Albert (1969) in a study that compared board members in failing and succeeding United Funds. It is not known how long such a cycle will endure or what might cause such spiralling to run down eventually.

Assumption: Members of a failing group make more attempts to reduce their group-oriented embarrassment when conditions heighten their sensitivity to the effects of failure.

When a group has repeatedly failed, the members' shame and their efforts to reduce these feelings will vary from time to time and place to place. It is likely that these variations will be due, broadly speaking, to conditions that make members more interested in their group's fate or more sensitive to increased embarrassment. Let us consider several predictions in the next four hypotheses.

Hypothesis: A member will more actively attempt to reduce group-oriented embarrassment if he is more concerned about the fate of his group.

Different kinds of circumstances may cause a participant to have a stronger interest in how well his unit performs. Among these conditions is the degree of centrality or peripherality in the person's job. We assume that a more central person will be more involved in his group. Some support for the above hypothesis was reported by Medow and Zander (1965), who experimentally varied the centrality or peripherality of members' roles. When a person was in a central position, he was more realistic about how well his group was doing and was more attentive to reducing embarrassment after his group had failed. When a member was in a peripheral post, he paid little attention to the objective facts of the group's situation and did not accept a failure as a failure.

A number of research findings support the hypothesis that more involved members work harder to reduce their chagrin over a group's failure. Table 1 lists several conditions that seem to arouse more (or less) concern about reducing the effects of group failure. The middle column indicates which condition is known to be, or assumed to be, more conducive to such coping actions.

Table 1. Group Conditions Conducive to Coping with Embarrassment

Variable	*Condition Most Conducive to Coping Behavior*	*Reference*
1. Desire for group success (Dgs) vs. Desire to avoid group failure (Dgaf)	Dgs > Dgaf	Zander and Ulberg, 1971
2. Perceived ability of group colleagues	Able > Inept	Zander, Fuller, and Armstrong, 1972
3. Size of group	Small > Large	
4. Unity of group	Strong Unity > Weak Unity	Zander, Stotland, and Wolfe, 1960
5. Degree of consensus on goal for group	Strong > Weak	Forward, 1969
6. Opportunity to discuss feelings about group	Available > Not Available	Zander, 1971
7. Cohesiveness of group	Strong > Weak	
8. Cooperation vs. Competition	Cooperation > Competition	

Obviously, a group that better involves its members is more eager to reduce group-oriented embarrassment. When members are less involved they are less affected by the group's failure and thus less concerned about reducing such embarrassment.

Hypothesis: Members of a group will more actively attempt to reduce group-oriented embarrassment when nonmembers provide a standard of excellence for the group.

A work group seldom has a task that interests its members and no one else. Ordinarily, its product is useful to outsiders, whether the outsiders are superiors, customers, advisers, or other people. These nonmembers may try to get the group to improve its performance or set a harder goal. We can sensibly anticipate that members will be more embarrassed and will try harder to reduce that embarrassment when their group fails to perform as well as outside agents have asked of it.

Several studies illustrate how members react when their group is put under pressure by sources in its environment. Zander and Curtis (1965) noted that members in failing units displayed more adaptive activity when their groups were provided with standards about how well they were expected to perform than when they were provided with no standards at all. Coping with embarrassment was more common in another study (Zander and Ulberg, 1971) when the demands of individuals outside the group were more suitable to the members' plans at the moment than when they were not.

Social pressures exerted by certain external agents are more acceptable, of course, than pressures by others. We suspect that a group's readiness to reduce a sense of humiliation will be considerably stronger when the members have greater respect for, or admiration for, the one who expects them to do well.

Hypothesis: Members of a group will make more attempts to reduce group-oriented embarrassment when it has failed on an easy task than when it has failed on a hard one.

We remarked earlier that dissatisfaction and shame are greater when a group fails on an easy task than when it fails on a hard one. If that is correct, it should be possible to obtain support for this hypothesis.

Hypothesis: Members of a group will make more attempts to reduce group-oriented embarrassment if their own self-regard is greater.

In some units certain members are confident of their own value, skill, or contribution in the group even though the organization as a whole is not performing well. The opposite also occurs: Some members know they are inept and know they contribute to a poor score in their group. The hypothesis suggests that persons with stronger self-esteem pay more attention to reducing embarrassment over the group's outcome than embarrassment over their own part. Those with low self-esteem are predicted to pay more attention to their own personal condition than the group's.

A number of findings which suggest that we may find support for this hypothesis are summarized in Table 2.

Table 2. Personal Qualities Conducive to Coping with Group Embarrassment

Characteristic of Member	*Conditions Most Conducive to Coping Behavior*	*Reference*
1. Hope for success (Ms) vs. Fear of failure (Maf)	Ms > Maf	Zander, 1971
2. Ego strength	Strong > Weak	Thomas and Zander, 1959
3. Individual competence on assignment for group	High > Low	Zander and Wulff, 1966
4. Centrality of role of group	Central > Peripheral	Medow and Zander, 1965 Zander, Forward, and Albert, 1969
5. Desire group to have a harder goal	Strong > Weak	Zander and Medow, 1963

Thus, two broad interests affect a member's tendency to reduce group-oriented embarrassment: how strongly the individual is involved in the fate of his group and the amount of confidence a member has in himself. Efforts to adapt to group-oriented embarrassment will be stronger as these two conditions are stronger.

Summary

After a group has resoundingly failed, the members may try either of two things: plan how the unit can improve so that it will be successful in the future or seek to reduce embarrassment caused by the group's poor performance. Because of the group's recent failure, members will place more weight on reducing their embarrassment than on ensuring the group's success because there is a better chance of lowering embarrassment than there is of attaining success. The actions usually taken to reduce embarrassment do little, however, toward ensuring a future success, and thus a group that focuses on lowering embarrassment will probably generate embarrassment again.

Chapter Six

Preventing Inefficient Meetings

Devotees of committee meetings know that some sessions go more smoothly than others. In certain instances participants talk freely and collaborate easily while moving toward a decision they quickly accept. In other groups, participants are guarded, their flow of discussion wanders, and they interfere with one another while attempting to reach a solution. In the latter case, chairpersons have a hard time getting ideas out of members and using those ideas that do come forth. As a result, the group's discussion does not follow the typical steps in solving a problem and the group's efficiency is low. Members work longer and accomplish less.

We are interested in groups that must arrive at a good-quality decision within a reasonable length of time and thus cannot afford to lose their way or dawdle during meetings. In this chapter we shall focus on problems in a group's process that are caused by unsure coordination of their efforts, trying to answer the questions "How can procedural awkwardness be prevented?" and "What tools and procedures have been invented for this purpose?"

There are many ways in which a group's problem can be relieved by a method specifically geared for solving that problem. One method is the parliamentary rules of order, which prevent group members from meandering or skipping from topic to topic. And a group's disinterest in a particular topic can be overcome by breaking the group into subsets, giving these subunits special questions to answer. A "science court" (Kantrowitz and others, 1976) that would establish which facts are correct among those brought to bear on a technological issue (for example, the effects of freon gas on the atmosphere) has been proposed. Officials' desire to give citizens a more "meaningful" part in a decision of a governmental agency inspired a report by a task group on how to foster citizen participation (1976).

Procedural difficulties in decision-making bodies deserve attention from social engineers because ways to relieve these problems are badly needed. The current methods have not been studied to see if they work: Are they really helpful, or merely ingenious? Developments in social technology can, moreover, provide insights into what leads to what (during meetings), so that basic research into groups may be enriched and stimulated. Because we will be considering here a number of procedures and technical inventions provided by social engineers as solutions to practical problems in group meetings, there is no single issue, as there is in other chapters, to be explained by a simple theory. Thus, instead of examining basic assumptions and related hypotheses we shall merely observe that there is a need for studies to evaluate the effectiveness of these procedures and tools.

Procedural difficulties interfere with the efficiency of a decision-making group. We shall consider three familiar kinds and suggest preventives for them: (1) insufficient interaction among participants, (2) confusion caused by varied views among members, and (3) difficulty in making an urgent decision in the face of a crisis. What can be proposed for the alleviation of such problems? If special practices prevent or heal these maladies, it should be possible to cure others as well.

Factors Inhibiting Interaction Among Members

Recall a meeting in which talking was infrequent or hesitant, participants chose their words with care and spoke only on certain topics, and only a few persons at the table talked freely. Or take a session in which the chairperson asked for comments from members and received silence. In such gatherings, participants are not calling upon the talents, information, or curiosity they bring with them; when that is the case, the quality of the group's decision is lowered. Reasonably competent participants become less competent when conditions cause them to be overly careful.

Why is a member timid during a meeting? One reason is that he may fear that what he says will not help the group move toward completion of its task or that he will waste the time of colleagues who listen to his comment and weigh its merits. A member also may hold back because she is apprehensive about being disapproved by others. Such disparagement of her is more likely, and self-inhibition more frequent, if she has unpleasant things to say to others. This is the result of the MUM effect we discussed in Chapter 2 (Rosen, 1970). If her ideas are deviant from the established views of members, her notions may be given little value by colleagues, who may even threaten her with rejection from the group because of her beliefs (Festinger, 1950). She may have been ridiculed earlier for things she said publicly, and now she holds her tongue to avoid a repetition of that experience. A member may suspect there is a danger of retaliation by powerful superiors if he says something that opposes them. Or, he may feel that he cannot trust others, he is vulnerable to them, and they can abuse that vulnerability and cause penalties to be greater than gains for him. Zand (1972) showed that when lack of trust exists among colleagues, an individual will conceal information that might increase his exposure to other persons, and at the same time he will provide inaccurate, narrow, or untimely information about himself. Thus, a member may decide to speak only when spoken to, and then to say no more than is necessary.

Another cause for discomfort and constrained participation is an adversary relationship among members. This condition may not limit the frequency of oral participation, but it may reduce the quality of the comments because members do not think before they speak, do not attend to the things others say, and may make coercive remarks to one another. Such defensive behavior occurs in meetings of labor versus management, philosophers versus scientists, and Arabs versus Jews (Levi and Benjamin, 1976). In short, when tension among participants is high because of cultural or background differences, members try to influence others but do not accept influence from them. The oral contributions are no more useful than no comments at all. These causes of difficulty in a group suggest what preventive measures may be worthy of study.

1. Prohibit face-to-face interaction. The chances that a person will be uncomfortable in a group can be considerably minimized if he does not have to talk with others because, when separated from them, he will not see evidence of disparagement, ridicule, or hostility toward him. Instead of face-to-face discussion, participants might be asked to sit at a table with other members and write private comments about a number of issues posed by the chairperson. This procedure, called the "nominal group technique" (Delbecq, Van de Ven, and Gustafson, 1975), takes advantage of the social facilitation created by the mere presence (and silence) of others. Later, the written comments might be shared aloud, publicly listed, and openly discussed. Or, two sets of members may meet in different rooms during a discussion period and come together after they have had a chance to consider the stated views of the other group. This procedure is especially useful when one group is higher in status than the other. Interaction by members may also be via paper, as in the Delphi method. In this procedure the members

complete a questionnaire about their opinions, and the results are reported to participants as part of a second questionnaire, in which members are now asked to react to the former results. Such feedback and further questioning continues on various issues. Still another method is to instigate face-to-face discussion in several small groups, each group in a separate room composed of individuals who are comfortable with one another. The results of each group's discussion are periodically shared, in writing, until the smaller groups feel ready for meeting jointly. Blake, Mouton, and Sloma (1965) describe an experience in which members of a union and members of a management refused to talk to those in the other unit for many months. The authors aroused a willingness for the two sides to talk. First, each unit (in a separate room) listed its perceptions of the countergroup on newsprint; these lists were then shared. Next, each group listed its guesses as to why the countergroup felt as it did. These lists were again shared. These procedures continued until the members in the two groups could no longer contain their desire to understand the others (pro or con) and to explain their own views. The communication gap was thus overcome at their own behest.

2. Provide anonymity in interaction. Another way to forestall unpleasant interpersonal relationships is to guarantee individuals anonymity when they are voting. For instance, the members may be asked to use an electronic balloting machine that reveals how many votes there are for a given proposition without indicating who voted which way. Sheridan (1975) described an electronic device that lets all members of a discussion group report to the chairperson simultaneously and secretly how they feel about a given issue. The participants may have as many as ten alternatives to choose from (the alternatives have been identified earlier during the group's discussion). The results of this vote are then displayed, and members again return to discussion until they are ready to vote once more. Sheridan said that this procedure provides a means of focusing quickly on how members feel about an issue, determining on which matters there is consensus, involving everyone in the room anonymously, letting the agenda be guided by the group, talking about issues without knowing for sure who favors what, and pre-

venting any embarrassment that may arise from open confrontation or disagreement. The Delphi procedure also provides anonymity, as does a computer when it is used in conferring.

3. Disallow evaluative comments. It takes less machinery to forbid oral appraisal of anything that is said in a meeting. This is the typical ground rule in so-called brainstorming sessions. The rationale is that all discussants will speak more freely, and perhaps imaginatively, if they know that overt reactions to their observations are prohibited, temporarily at least.

In an unpublished paper, Hepp (1975) postulated that people in marginal countries hold back in group efforts because they have little confidence in what they can achieve by that means. Hepp described a kind of discussion method he used to help a group set an important and attainable goal, as the members saw it. He also asked members to describe successes they had; these successes were then praised. The result was that members began to talk more freely and boldly and to develop faith in their group's chances of success.

4. Generate interdependence among members. Frequency of intermember talk can be increased by making members dependent on each other for achievement of individual and joint goals (Deutsch, 1973). If members have a common goal, clearly silence is unwise, as is any slowdown of effort. The more important the joint goal, the more members will actively collaborate to achieve it.

5. Reduce the strength of pressures toward uniformity. Every group develops standards about how it will do its work and about the issues members believe are important for their unit's survival. Colleagues require conformity to these standards by exerting on one another social pressures toward uniformity. These social pressures cause a constraint on both the frequency of participation and the innovativeness of ideas because members are pressed to adhere to the group's standard whenever they show signs of deviating from it in thought or deed. Janis (1972) referred to this effect as "groupthink" and showed that better solutions may be rejected by a group in favor of poorer ones simply because the former are too different from the group's fixed practices.

Preventing Inefficient Meetings

Janis proposed several techniques members may use to prevent groupthink or to weaken pressures toward uniformity: assign the role of critical evaluator to each member; ask each member to discuss the group's deliberations with trusted associates outside the group and report back their reactions; assign one member the role of devil's advocate; examine the desires and intentions of members with views that are known to conflict with the present group's preferences; and, once a decision is reached, have the group, at a later meeting, closely consider all residual doubts about the proposed solution.

There are other methods for helping members overcome inhibitions during a discussion. The topic might be made more attractive by stressing its relevance to the fate of members in the group or to the group as a unit; the chairperson might be highly supportive of members so they feel safe to try out their ideas in public; or the members might be told that persons outside the present group need a decision from them.

Reducing Confusion Among Members with Varied Views

Recently I sat in several meetings that were to develop a single set of plans from a variety of ideas. In one case, the question was how to finance the purchase of a computer that, in time, would pay for itself through the endeavors of the decision makers. In a series of meetings, the officers of a small company were to decide what products should be kept in their line and what ones should be dropped. In a third instance, we were to propose the policies that would govern budgets for research projects. In each case members offered notions that did not fit together well. At times, in fact, these ideas were conflicting. But the conflicts were seldom two sided, as is usually assumed in theories about social conflict. Rather, there were varied disagreements, with various disagreers, at various periods. Differing views were often expressed in unique terms, which added to the welter of ideas on the table.

A major effect of these contrasting beliefs and shifts in alliance was confusion on several matters. The confusion concerned what issue is under discussion, what information is most salient to that issue, what solutions are being suggested, and how good these solutions are. At times the members simply did not know what was being discussed, or where they were on the path toward a solution. Can a complex task be simplified so such confusion is minimized? In principle, simplification is possible through procedures that develop orderliness of effort. The following measures merit study as means to divert confusion.

1. Find a focus of interest. A logical way to simplify a discussion is to choose the most attractive topic among the alternatives available. This can be done in several ways. A common approach is to ask individuals to rank in order a number of subjects according to their perceived value. This method is not always the happiest because it requires discussants to accept the issue that receives the highest average rating, these orderings are difficult to make when many topics are available, and the reasons that one topic is preferred over another may be lost to the discussion. It is somewhat easier for members to rate the attractiveness of each of the suggested topics on a simple scale.

Members will usually be interested in the reasons why colleagues prefer a given topic. Accordingly, Levi and Benjamin (1976) suggested a procedure that taps this information. They asked participants to select their preferred subject from among a list and to give the reasons for this preference. The remaining members were then invited to rate the importance of each reason—where importance means the strength of the desire to have that reason fulfilled. Members chose the topic on which there was the least disagreement and the most promise of satisfaction.

A heated discussion will generate confusion for participants simply because the disagreers are not able, in the midst of the argument, to gather and organize their thoughts: They interfere with one another's thinking, and what they say they do not say well, or anger causes the members to sit in grim silence. Varelo (1971) proposed that a chairperson, in such a situation, call for a period of quiet, during which the members are to summarize the discussion in writing and suggest a next step. Or, such a group may be broken temporarily into pairs or trios of discussants who consider these matters orally in their small sets. Several scholars have written extensively about the constructive consequences when subgroups work through a conflict in separate settings (Blake, Mouton, and Sloma, 1965; Chevalier, Bailey, and Burns, 1975; Delbecq, Van de Ven, and Gustafson, 1975).

A focus of interest may be easier to identify for the members, or a degree of disagreement may be easier to handle, if the decision-making body is composed of persons who in the past have participated in groups that had lively differences within them and were able to tolerate and reason through these dissimilar views. Sometimes a chairperson has the opportunity to select a set of individuals and teach them how to work together.

2. Follow a strict sequence of procedural steps. Confusion that arises because members cannot tell where they are in movement toward a solution ought to be preventable. Imagine a discussion leader who explains the phases that must be accomplished, one after the other, to reach a decision. The chairperson thereafter makes sure the members are aware of the phase they occupy at that moment and limits their comments to ones which fit the current phase. The chairperson helps members move to the next phase when they are ready for that. A "shaped" group discussion (Maier, 1963) illustrates this form, as does the Program Evaluation and Review Technique, commonly called PERT (Cook, 1966). Sheridan (1975) described a process he calls "branching," in which members periodically vote, anonymously, on what issues they wish to consider next and what ones they wish to ignore.

The sequential parts of a discussion, if they are identified ahead of time, can be tightly followed, and leadership methods that will prevent deviation from them can be used. Strict guidance of this type is inherent in the Delphi procedure and in many of the programs developed for use of the computer during a conference (Paines, Hench, and Zinn, 1976). Do these procedures improve the efficiency of a decision process? Because they are precise moves, that question ought to be answerable.

3. Follow a strict set of rules. A procedure similar to the one

just mentioned, but a bit more elaborate, is the use of rules that have been drawn up ahead of time; examples are rules followed in labor-management negotiations, parliamentary practices, or rules of order. The intention of such legislation is to provide a group with an approved method for preventing confusion or for extricating itself from chaos when many ideas beg for consideration at once. One rule that often can make others unnecessary is to set a time limit for the discussion—when time is precious, members discipline themselves more effectively, I think. This observation is worthy of study.

4. Give decision-making power to a central person. Many societies have formal customs for choosing among disparate views. In one approach advocates of each approach present their arguments and respond to the others' statements before a passive judge, referee, or arbitrator. This official then decides who is right. Sometimes a small group takes the place of this wise person. In a contrasting approach, advocates are silent until addressed by the central character, who questions and probes them until he is ready to render his decision. In either case, a strong person decides.

The science court, proposed by Kantrowitz and others (1976), is a close relative of such time-honored schemes, except that the court is not a decision-making or policy-setting body. Rather, it is a problem-solving group that determines which ones, among a set of contradictory scientific "facts," are correct. The judge or judges in this kind of court are scientists themselves. Critics of the science court fear that the reports issued by it will not properly consider the values that ought to have a part in an evaluation. Thus, Hammond and Adelman (1976) proposed a specific step-by-step procedure for amalgamating scientific data in one setting, and value judgments in a different setting, to help on an adversary discussion. A third group then decides what should be done. In the case study Hammond and Adelman discuss, to illustrate their views, community citizens and city officials decide what kind of bullets the local police should use, and why.

A common practice in negotiations between union and management representatives is to use a third party when progress in bargaining has stalled. It is understood that the opposing sides ordinarily will reach agreements unaided. When that fails, however, they may ask for advice, not a decision, from a person called a mediator. If the mediator is no help, they can turn to an arbitrator, who will make a ruling that is binding on both sides. All three steps—bargaining, mediating, and arbitrating—are governed by rules with the weight of law. All three steps, moreover, must be performed in good faith. Can these steps be used in problems with many sides?

In the measures we have been reviewing in the last few paragraphs, a central person, usually a third party, is given the right to settle the differences when varied views exist. The basic ideas inherent in the measures are applicable to any meeting, but they are seldom used in settings outside those described because they demand planning ahead of time, trained personnel to carry them out, and money.

Chevalier, Bailey, and Burns (1975) showed how a focal person, whom they called a manager of planning, is necessary for integrating the ideas of separate groups engaged in long-range thinking. This manager identifies similarities in the goals and common concerns among separate units and thereby helps such units develop a collective involvement. Quinn and Major (1974) believed that separate committees, each concerned with planning for some aspect of the future, developed sounder goals and ones that fitted together better when these objectives were chosen by a central group, not by the different committees themselves. Finally, Stone (1975) suggested that the boards of large corporations may be monitored (to ensure that they give weight to needs of society, as well as to profit for the company) by a board director who is chosen by citizens and is charged with representing their wishes.

5. Reduce barriers caused by time and space. It is not always convenient or feasible to bring to a table all those who ought to discuss a given topic. Accordingly, engineers interested in communication have worked on ways of reducing the barriers created by physical separation. They have developed the means, as an example, for conducting a conference with the help of a computer (Paines, Hench, and Zinn, 1976). In this method a conferee seats

himself at a terminal, whenever it suits his schedule to do so, and requests a print-out of messages that have accumulated from any or all of the other conferees (who also occasionally sit at their own terminals) on any or all relevant topics. He then may type into the record his own responses or comments. The computer provides a means for storage and selection of this information in such a way that conferencing can occur over any distance, among any number of persons, for as long a period as they wish to exchange ideas. Do participants take the time to read and type these messages? Can they discuss abstract ideas in this way? Do they get tired of this method? How many persons have such gadgetry available for their use? How many people have the knowledge and skills necessary to use this expensive machinery? The telephone company knows that many customers do not dare make a long distance call because they fear it is too complicated to do so. Likewise, few ordinary folks may have the courage to use a terminal and computer for conferencing.

A simpler procedure is the conference telephone call, in which each of a number of individuals, on a party line, can hear any of the others. Etzioni (1975) tried to make improvements on the methods for holding these conversations. He and his colleagues installed picturephones at each station, reasoning that seeing the faces of other members would make an electronic meeting more like a face-to-face gathering. They were surprised to learn that the picturephones were not very feasible because the cameras were too often pointed in the wrong direction, and the cost was fantastically high. Etzioni and others also ran a number of simple telephone conferences with no picturephones to study the properties of such meetings. Some problems were hard to handle. How can a member transmit to the chairperson a request for the floor? How can the chairperson prevent several persons from talking at once? How can a participant transmit cues to others about her feelings? (This is done by gestures and postures when people are together.) How can a member be sure who is talking? How can the chairperson control a wandering discussion?

To investigate some of these problems, Etzioni and his associates developed a cue-box that allowed a discussant to signal the leader that he wanted the floor and allowed him to show (via one or another color of light) how he felt about what was being said by discussants. This device did not help members much because it flooded them with more information than they could handle. Which light, for example, belonged to whom? The prime conclusion among these experiments was that small telephone conferences work better than large ones because they are less subject to confusion.

6. Allow members to practice for their meeting. We have been implying that group members and chairpersons can learn to minimize confusion. If that implication is valid, it would be sensible to plan and rehearse for a potentially chaotic meeting. One way to anticipate a session is to ask participants (or their surrogates) to take part in a simulated meeting prior to the real one. In this miniature version of war games, the discussants play the roles they will have in the real discussion at a later time. Observers, with the help of the members themselves, thereupon analyze the nature of the difficulties the unit can expect to meet when the discussion is for keeps, and they can plan what they might do to improve the group's procedures. This kind of rehearsal has been effective in meetings on community problems, where opposing sides exist. Indeed, the Extension Service of The University of Michigan provides an advisory service that helps local citizens conduct a simulation game about their community problems. Here is a true preventive measure.

Need for a Rapid Decision

A crisis in an organization (or a larger community) typically requires joint decision making by a number of persons; one person alone can seldom handle it. In contrast to a routine problem, a crisis (according to Kupperman, Wilcox, and Smith, 1975) is accompanied by a sense of urgency and a concern that the situation is becoming worse in the absence of effective remedial action. This concern is the source of the need for haste. A number of things need to be done—all of them at once.

The central problems in dealing with crises are caused by

poor communication among those individuals who must decide and act and difficulty in providing quickly whatever may be needed (resources, plans, approvals). Several aspects of these issues are worthy of consideration because they suggest ways of reducing their impact.

To solve any problem, data and other forms of information are needed. When the problem is an emergency, these facts and ideas must be obtained quickly. But the changing (or potentially worsening) situation itself makes it hard to get facts at all, let alone current and changing ones. Concerned persons want to know what is happening now? Soon? Later? These questions are hard to answer because the data needed for a response may not be delivered in a usable form. As a result of this paucity of good information, decision makers must depend on their past experience or their intuition about what they ought to do.

A crisis, according to Kupperman and colleagues, causes different people to respond in different ways and leads them to place contrasting pressures on the individuals who are to make the decisions. These persons may, for example, disagree about what should be done first to prevent deterioration of the situation, given that some actions are more central than others. Certain members will be worried about potential deprivations to themselves or to their department and will press for solutions that will take care of these early on. If the situation does in fact change for the worse, plans must be modified, and these changes will require a new set of priorities. Finally, the tension generated by haste and prolonged attention leads to fatigue that, in turn, causes less effective action.

What methods can speed up the process of decision making? Those that ought to work here are remarkably similar to those that should reduce confusion. The difference is that they need to be done more expeditiously. Kupperman and others think that a crisis can best be handled by centralizing all decision making because one, or a very few persons, can best keep track of events and most quickly decide what must be done.

Wars, hurricanes, and other disasters demand rapid and wise planning. The decision makers in such settings often practice how to meet these emergencies. Similarly, organizations can experiment ahead of time with ways of increasing their speed in making decisions and in altering the ways based on subsequent experience. Most hospitals and utility companies have prepared procedures for meeting excessive and urgent demands for their services; other kinds of groups could do this as well.

The fact is, we know little about the procedural problems that arise for a group when it must move rapidly. In the absence of such information, we do not have many good ideas about how to make urgent meetings effective ones. These problems are worthy of further study.

Summary

Procedural problems in a group can be relieved by inventions that prevent these problems, or overcome their unwanted effects. A variety of inventions can be used; some of the inventions have been tried out, whereas others have the status of bright ideas. Almost none of these measures have been evaluated to determine if they have the effects they ought to have. Such evaluative studies are overdue. Three kinds of procedural problems are worthy of attention: (1) insufficient open interaction among participants, (2) confusion created by varied views among members, and (3) difficulty in making an urgent decision to meet a deteriorating situation.

Chapter Seven

Vulnerability of the Modern Manager

In every field of endeavor there are individuals who strive for excellence, whether they be artists, athletes, coaches, crooks, performers, salespeople, scientists, or writers. And among administrators it is not surprising that some try to become well skilled in the things they must do and try to live up to the best practices of the day. These managers tend to be sophisticated, intelligent, and conscientious persons who are aware of the qualities a good administrator should have and are willing to shape their behavior to suit those standards.

I have known excellent administrators in the military, government, business, and education who have strived to attain excellence. I have observed their behavior on the job and have heard them talk about what they are trying to do and why. (Most of these managers work in university settings but, so far as I can see, there is remarkably little difference in administrative problems and behaviors in these separate situations.) Because they do what they consider best, a number of these managers have similar ideas about what is required of them and have similar problems in attaining excellence, particularly in their relations with subordinates.

Unfortunately, the attempts of managers to live up to modern doctrines of good management sometimes are the cause of interpersonal difficulties. The evidence I can cite about such difficulties is qualitative and anecdotal. I made notes when I saw managers face problems that writings about management or leadership seldom if ever discuss. Yet these are prime problems for managers that are worthy of study by specialists in administrative behavior; in fact, some problems have been exacerbated by the writings of manager-scholars. In this chapter we shall assume that there are several forms of "good practice" in current managerial circles. The notions behind these habits are widely known, accepted by many managers, and followed closely by a fair proportion of them. We are interested in persons who believe in these practices and try to live up to them.

Good Managerial Practices

Assumption: A good manager encourages participative management.

One style of management emphasizes joint problem solving and decision making by some or all persons who are relevant to the problem under study and tries to involve representatives from different levels of the hierarchy when that makes sense. This type of management also gives considerable attention to the rights of colleagues and to rules for due process, especially in decisions about the careers of organizational members. Synonyms for this approach are team management, power equalization, system four, human resources management, and organic management.

Almost twenty years ago, Likert (1959) and McGregor (1959) noted that managers were developing an increasing interest and skill in this managerial style. More recently, Halal (1974) reviewed a number of studies which demonstrated to him that this pattern of administration has continued to increase in popularity and will do so in the future. An important reason for support of this good practice is that managers are pressed to encourage wider participation in decision making by the demands of unions, civil rights laws, and profit-sharing methods and interest in industrial democracy, rules enforcing full employment, and the increase in skill among employees in litigation. A different reason for using participative management is that the performance of an organization can be improved if those who do its work bring their experiences directly to bear in planning for this work. A wise manager, moreover, recognizes that the motives of subordinates are likely to be stronger if the members have a chance to influence decisions, particularly if these decisions serve the members' needs.

It should be noted that the demands of this good practice fall more strongly on a superior than on a subordinate. The superior must allow his subordinates to have some degree of social influence before this kind of management can work. The superior is the gatekeeper. Thus, conformity to this good practice places a requirement on the higher status person but only an opportunity before the lower status one. The superior must, the subordinate merely can—if he wishes to do so. Should the subordinate not want to participate, out of boredom or ineptness, he does not have to take part. Subordinates may even press their superiors to conform to this good practice while not demanding participation for themselves.

Assumption: A good manager treats a subordinate in a way that respects a member's dignity and desires.

Participative management requires a manager to be insightful, supportive, and helpful toward her subordinates, rather than excessively assertive. In her attempts to influence subordinates, the administrator is to use expert information and logic rather than sanctions. She should encourage subordinates to develop a sense of autonomy on the job and make it possible for them to improve their knowledge and skills. A superior member is to treat subordinates as though their desires are worthy of attention. This, in turn, is a natural corollary of today's emphasis on shared decision making based on egalitarianism and democratic values. Writers about management in the last twenty years often claim that managers who follow these two practices are more effective. Although there is little confirming evidence pro or con on the effectiveness of managers who adhere to this style, many administrators believe these procedures work well for them.

Assumption: An administrator's major responsibility is to keep the organization functioning well.

This is not merely a good practice the manager may or may not follow as he wishes; it is a prime duty that allows him no choice. In contrast to others, some managers have a stronger desire to work in behalf of the organization. Our guess is that a superior's desire for group success increases as others expect her to be more concerned about the fate of the organization because:

1. The superior's duties involve her in the productivity of the unit instead of, say, personal counseling.
2. Her role is a more responsible or central one rather than a less responsible or peripheral one.
3. The manager is pressed by agents outside the organization, such as shareholders, unions, clients, or customers, to attend to the organization's performance.
4. She is more satisfied by the success of the organization than by her own achievements.
5. She is unusually competent in the tasks she must perform for the organization.

A modern manager must also enforce many demands laid on the unit by persons who are not part of the organization. These demands affect the unit's reputation in the world and determine what the manager must demand of himself and others. The requirements derive from special interests like women's rights, rights of ethnic groups and minorities, pollution control, Internal Revenue Service rules, unemployment compensation, social security, standards for pension funds, labor relations laws, guidelines for handling toxic substances, health and safety regulations, consumer complaints, fair advertising controls, postal regulations, and so on. Ironically, a manager who is pressed to see that her subordinates adhere to these external demands is typically blamed as a source and advocate of these rules. Thus, the more the group must deal with external rules, the harder it is for a manager to follow good practices—powerful regulatory agencies can spoil good managers.

Effects of Good Managerial Practices

Any administrator who accepts these good practices and tries to abide by them may meet conditions that modify the effects of his actions. Let us examine a few of these conditions by the following two hypotheses.

Hypothesis: Many of a good manager's practices concern matters initiated by his subordinates.

One who adheres to the first two assumptions must provide time for the consideration of topics suggested by individuals at lower, as well as higher, levels in the hierarchy. Look at the agenda of an administrative committee. Many of the items are of interest to subordinates, and quite a few have been proposed by those who will be affected by the decision. Examine the memos or mail a manager receives from his colleagues, hear the telephone calls he gets, or sit in the corner of his office while visitors drop in to see him. Often what is said at these times is initially suggested by the lower-status person and is more important to that person than to the manager. The initiator may need advice, help, permission, approval, sympathy, money, or access to persons in other parts of the organization. He approaches the superior for help to do or get those things.

The tendency for communication to flow upward more than downward in a hierarchy was noted in both laboratory experiments and natural settings (Cartwright and Zander, 1968a). But none of the various motives offered for this phenomenon have been wholly convincing. For our purposes it is sufficient to recognize that subordinates will direct more communication toward the superior than vice versa because there are many subordinates who can send messages, but only one superior. This excludes, of course, broad managerial pronouncements that are intended to affect all receivers in a similar way. Any manager can send out many such pronouncements, but so can a subordinate if he is inclined to do so. However, the subordinate is seldom so inclined because his crucial interest is in the messages to, and the action by, his boss.

Administrators differ, as persons, in what may be called their approachability, that is, their likelihood of welcoming and acting favorably on requests for action rather than rejecting or disapproving them. A more approachable administrator, a better follower of good practices, is likely to receive more communication from subordinates. This hypothesis has been supported in empirical studies (Cartwright and Zander, 1968a). We can anticipate, although there are no objective data on the matter, that members of an organization who place more value on participative management will engage in more upwardly directed communication and that persons who support the values of participation will probably be more approachable as well.

We can thus deduce that many of the actions taken by a manager are to meet problems or issues which were not initially her concern. She often is responding to a stimulus and grants, permits, allows, suggests, urges, helps, or forbids matters that have been put before her at others' behests, not her own. She is a reactor more than an initiator.

Hypothesis: Topics sent up to a manager for action are more likely to emphasize desires of the sender, or her immediate peers, than the needs of the organization as a whole.

Because, as suggested, the initiator is asking for action by one who is powerful, her request will probably concern some matter of central importance to her. All else equal, the content of the request will be closer to determining the fate of the initiator than not; it will certainly be closer to her personal activities than to those of the larger organization. There is some evidence to support this hypothesis (Zander, 1971).

Assumption: Given the demands a manager must enforce for the good of his organization, he is bound to disapprove of certain matters originated by his subordinates.

This assumption recognizes the desires of the subordinate and the duties of the superior, as well as the poor fit that may occur between them. No one, superior or subordinate, can regularly have his own way in the decisions being made for the good of that unit. Where good practices are followed, there may be more decisions acceptable to all simply because there will have been more active give and take among members of that unit, and there may, as a result, be a more common view among all concerned. Accordingly, perhaps followers of good managerial practice less often have to turn down a subordinate's request than do those who are not followers of good practice. Given that the manager encourages his colleagues to take an active part in influencing decisions in the organization and that he tries to respect the dignity of the members, and given that the manager occasionally refuses a proposal or request from a subordinate, we may anticipate that a subordinate might react to the refusal in an assertive manner, as described in the next hypothesis.

Hypothesis: The more a manager follows good practice, the more a subordinate will exert social pressure on him to reverse a disapproval.

A "no" need not be taken as the final answer if the administrator has already demonstrated that he is open to the ideas of his colleagues. A disapproval may merely be a signal to the subordinate that there is a need for more discussion and more attempts to influence the disapprover. It should follow that a manager will more often reopen and reappraise his decisions when he is an adherent of modern good practice.

Hypothesis: The more a manager follows good practice, the less a subordinate will fear retaliation when he places pressure on the manager.

In a public meeting to review the decision procedures that had been employed in settling a controversial problem over a period of many months, a spokesman for one group said that he and his colleagues "knew that they were irritating persons in positions of authority. But," he added, "we also knew that they would not do anything to us even though they were being irritated." The subordinates trusted the superiors to act rationally, believed the superiors were cowed into passivity, or counted on the adherence of the manager to good practice.

One form of social pressure is the use of coercion by a subordinate. This typically is a verbal statement about steps the subordinate says she will take if the superior does not make an acceptable decision or remake an unfavorable decision. Examples of this form of communication are shown in the following slightly edited quotes from letters.

> *Letter 1:* I need hardly say that I am angry and disappointed with the decision stated in the penultimate paragraph of your letter, and . . . I will neither accept nor tolerate it. I also question its legality. . . . Is this an example of how casually you have considered the whole question?
>
> *Letter 2:* I have been driven to desperation. . . . So I am bluntly threatening you. Either I have [a piece of machinery] installed by [date given] or I will do everything I can to get back at you. I once thought I was quite powerless, but it is surprising what an angry mind can think of. [Five threats are then listed about publicity that will be given this event to colleagues, officials, and senators.]
>
> *Letter 3:* I came to you for assistance in this matter last year, and therefore expect you to be sensitive to the matter. I expect a written apology for your action as well as other assurances [then listed].

In a more sophisticated form of coercion, persons whose wishes have been frustrated try to generate guilt in the administrator by alleging that his actions are morally inferior because they violate values precious to the complainer and his peers (he is undemocratic, unhealthy, ungodly, anti-intellectual, and so forth). An additional tactic is for the frustrated one to assert that his values are better than the superior's.

It seems reasonable that subordinates who use these behaviors sense that adherents of good practice will not quickly punish actions by subordinates. Good managers know the complainers have a right to be heard, so a refusal to listen by superiors is not good form. And in some organizations subordinates see their assertive behavior toward authority figures as a sign of strength, the opposite as a sign of weakness, and believe that militancy is a social virtue which earns the approval of colleagues.

We can guess that a member is more likely to use coercive social pressure the more the frustrated issue is important to her. She is less likely to show this kind of reaction, in contrast, if the fate of the organization is so important that she is willing to put her own wants second. If the group's existence or the attainment of its objectives are being threatened, members are usually more ready to welcome a strong boss who engages in strong acts in the unit's behalf—even if these acts demand the sacrificing of personal needs (Mulder, Ritesema van Eck, and de Jong, 1971). It follows that in large and impersonal institutions, where members have less interest in the success of their unit, the coercive behavior we have been considering should occur more often.

Hypothesis: In the face of coercive acts by his colleagues, the manager who follows good practices remains courteous, understanding, and calm. He meets and treats coercive persons with dignity.

The code of the modern administrator asks him to be a rational problem solver. His own emotional reactions are irrelevant and are to be set aside in favor of behavior that will best help the organization. The manager must see that the unit's policies and rules are not violated and weakened. He must also listen to any person who has been hurt by his actions and who might now be complaining to him. He cannot, if he is a model manager, meet subordinate's fire with fire. He seldom can use coercion himself. When he does so he is disapproved by his peers and righteously denounced by his subordinates.

In practical terms, this means that the good manager must respond to a hostile or unfair action with one that is calm and cool. She briefly shows her anger if that will help solve the original problem and will protect the organization, but she does not if it is only for a personal catharsis or to punish the other. She ordinarily must not resort to sarcasm, humor, or any other sign that suggests the problem can be easily handled with just good will because such behavior will be seen as either hostile or careless. When on the telephone, or in a face-to-face conference, she watches her choice of words and lowers her voice at the end of a sentence. She admits her own boners and seeks ways of correcting them. In short, she keeps herself under control and extends the symbols of peace when she can.

The stress a modern manager must learn to handle is mainly caused, I believe, by this need for suppressing his reactions and the care he must take in preparing a constrained response to subordinates. Handling emotional behavior in a calm manner leads to reoccurring uneasiness about the solution he offers—it also eats at the attention he should give to other matters.

Hypothesis: The better the manager (the more he follows good practice), the better an actor he is.

A follower of good managerial practices does not push others around when his deepest desire may be to do so. He acts as is expected of him, not as he wishes to do. Thus he often dissembles, in a gentle way. He plays a role, many roles, every day. Even though his heart often is not behind the face he displays, he must take the part that is needed at the moment. There also are emotions he must occasionally show even though he is not naturally disposed to do so. On separate occasions he may be stern, gay, serious, supportive, ceremonial, angry, uplifting, encouraging, rewarding, and so on, as is demanded by the instance. A skilled manager can turn these emotions off, and on; they follow one another without pause. It is remarkable how well he can drop one role and take up another as needed. It is also striking how seldom he appears to be false in taking these varied positions, and how often he successfully buries personal attitudes that are not immediately pertinent. All members of an organization, to be sure, switch roles from time to time, just as the manager does. But the manager has more frequent demands upon him to do so than does the subordinate, and his actions are more telling for others.

Because a manager spends so much time working with people, his successes are more often derived from interpersonal relations than from other forms of achievement such as writing, creating, or integrating. Thus his greatest source of satisfaction will lie in his relationship with other persons, and this may in turn cause him to give further weight to the good practices we noted.

Summary

Managers who strive for excellence believe that good practice requires them to encourage participation of subordinates in decision making and to treat these colleagues with respect for their dignity. Effective managers are duty bound, moreover, to help their organizations perform well.

Given that many issues are initiated by subordinates, and that these issues often are resolved in ways that are not acceptable to the persons who raised them, the frustrated persons may attempt to coerce the manager into changing his mind. The manager is treated in this coercive manner because, apparently, subordinates do not fear retaliation from a superior who is a follower of good practice.

In his efforts to adhere to good practice, the manager endures considerable strain and must be a good actor who can conceal his feelings and behave in an appropriate fashion. The vulnerability of the modern manager, because of the demands placed upon him, has received too little attention from students of managerial behavior.

Chapter Eight

The Manager's Associate

At a weekly staff meeting I am interested in watching two persons because of their contrasting styles. One person offers comments about such things as the amount of production, changes in personnel, repairs of equipment, adequacy of supplies, corrections for snafus, and the like. This speaker answers questions briskly, promising to check on this, and to work on that, soon. He announces changes in procedure and asks for approval from the boss. The other person speaks less often and is seldom called upon by the chair. When he talks he reports progress in the developing of long-range plans, tells of studies he has under way, gives information about new laws, taxes, federal paperwork, or demands on the organization. He asks penetrating questions of his colleagues but seldom proposes actions unless he is invited to do so.

Away from the conference room, the contrast between these men continues. The first man talks with other workers, at his desk, down the hall, or on the telephone. He roams widely among his colleagues, asking questions, giving instructions telling what he wants, or watching them at work. The contrasting individual is alone a good part of each day, writing, dictating, calculating, studying. He attends many meetings but he spends little time in one-to-one conversations.

The first person, the one who gives attention to details, is a familiar type, often called a supervisor, foreman, chief, chairman, director, or dean. In the following pages we shall call him a supervisor. The latter type of person, who seldom concentrates on details, is less familiar and may be labeled an associate, assistant, assistant-to, deputy, counsellor, or staff aide. We shall refer to him as an associate.

Role of the Associate

There are noteworthy psychological features of an associate's job that, to my knowledge, have never been examined by students of behavior because scholars are more interested in investigating how each official influences those who report to him and how his subordinates react to his supervision. Most researchers forget that many occupants of a hierarchy have no subordinates at all. What are the qualities of an administrator who has no one to whom he may administer?

In order to rule out effects due to differences in status, let us assume that both the associate and the supervisor of interest to us are peers, have the same superior, have similar ranks in the hierarchy of their organization, and receive the same pay. We focus on the role of the associate, using the role of the supervisory peer as a basis for contrast.

We can take it for granted that the jobs of associate and

supervisor are different in three respects, described in the following three assumptions.

Assumption: An associate has a less precisely defined set of duties than does a supervisor.

The functions of an associate include such duties as conducting special studies, chairing review committees, serving on a special task force, analyzing social pressures, suggesting new policies, gathering the latest data, writing letters that require careful wording, advising on complicated issues, appearing at ceremonies, and substituting for the superior in meetings. The associate may also have routine responsibilities like tending special budgets, planning investments, searching for new talent, and monitoring adherence to regulations. In contrast, a supervisor may be engaged in setting goals for his department, organizing efforts of colleagues or subordinates and providing resources for them, or checking on their work. The pattern of his activities within these categories will be fairly well established.

The associate's assignments are likely to be indefinite and to need interpretation about what should be accomplished and how. The supervisor's responsibilities are clearer and may be stated in terms of standard operating procedures. The associate's assignments are often changed and require varied and flexible arrangements for their accomplishment. The supervisor's duties are regularized and routinized over a longer period. The associate thinks in theoretical terms or considers the common qualities in a class of events rather than worrying about certain objects or particular procedures. The supervisor is more concerned about specific items or particular occurrences. The associate's work is intended to suit any of a variety of situations under the surveillance of his superior. The supervisor devotes most of his attention to matters under his own immediate control. The associate is asked to think about what the future may bring; the supervisor is expected to be concerned about the here and now.

Assumption: An associate, compared to a supervisor, has a smaller proportion of his interactions with subordinates and a larger proportion with his manager.

An associate has no or few subordinates, so he has little opportunity to act as a boss for others, to be approached by many subordinates for help, or to be supported by them. He may meet infrequently with his manager, but the contacts he has with him are a good proportion of all the personal interactions he has at work. A supervisor, in contrast, has many meetings with many different persons, superiors, peers, and subordinates alike.

Assumption: An associate works more for the manager than for the organization, whereas a supervisor works more for the organization than for the manager.

Changes in an associate's portfolio of activities are usually made by the boss, and these changes tend to reflect shifts in problems the boss must face. The supervisor's responsibilities, unlike the associate's, require him to attend to the effectiveness of his workers. Because of the need for reasonably stable procedures for persons under his supervision, a supervisor's duties do not change very often. All in all, a boss decides more of an associate's activities than a supervisor's. When an associate attempts to advise or persuade his boss, he is more likely to comment on matters he has been invited to consider by that person. When a supervisor wishes to change the views of his boss, he takes up issues that concern the good of the organization.

Characteristics of the Associate

If these conditions describe how an associate's job differs from a supervisor's, twelve hypotheses can be proposed about the typical experiences of an individual occupying each of these roles, and about the kind of person to be found in them. Our first six hypotheses deal with the relationship of the associate to the rest of the organization. The seventh through tenth hypotheses consider the associate's self-image; the last two discuss the characteristics of associates and supervisors.

Hypothesis: An associate is more likely to be praised or blamed by his boss than by others in the organization, whereas a supervisor is more likely to be praised by others than by his boss.

A good part of an associate's work is prepared for an audience of one, and that small audience usually does not reveal the content of this work or the name of its author to anyone else. The associate, moreover, seldom talks with others about the private interests of his boss. As a consequence, he occupies a quiet harbor. When a manager occasionally makes the advice of the associate public, or acts on the basis of it, the supervisor is considered the sponsor of these notions, not the associate. And if the ideas are approved by the superior's colleagues, the superior is praised; if they are disapproved, the superior is blamed. The associate, in brief, is not readily available for public evaluation. His private efforts are appraised, almost exclusively, by the one who requested and received them: the boss. There are occasions, of course, when an associate's effort becomes visible: A report is circulated with his name on it, or he has an important part in some organizational action. In such an instance the associate may be subject to approval or attack by others. Even here, however, a public reaction to the associate will be attenuated because members of the organization recognize that his action has been initiated by, and accepted by, the associate's superior. The boss remains a target.

Hypothesis: An associate, compared to a supervisor, has less influence on his organization.

An associate's ideas cannot have much weight within his organization if his output is seldom seen or appraised. The situation of the supervisor is sharply contrasting; his efforts are clearly visible to those whom he attempts to influence as well as to others who learn of his actions. An associate is sometimes asked to substitute for his boss in executive meetings. If he enters a continuing group, he may find himself in the midst of a discussion that has already extended over several sessions. Because he appears late in these deliberations, he is not sure what has been said, what he can properly say, or what he should say. As often as not, any remarks the associate offers are not quite appropriate in the context of the group's past discussion. He soon decides, therefore, that it is wisest for him to keep quiet. Those at the table observe that he has nothing to say and conclude he is incompetent. The more often he substitutes, the more his reputation suffers.

Hypothesis: There are more demands to abolish the associate's job than to abolish the supervisor's job.

As we remarked, an associate's work, in contrast to that of a supervisor, is not widely known. As a result, the associate's job is a suitable target for derogation when members complain that there are too many administrators (a common complaint in organizations). An associate, like a butler or a chauffeur, is considered a luxury if funds are scarce. An associate's location within the organization, moreover, is such that he will usually not hear about suggestions to abolish his job—and he will not pay attention to such news should it reach his ears.

Hypothesis: An associate, compared to a supervisor, is less likely to be promoted.

Because an associate may be perceived by colleagues to be of little use to the organization and in a job that is not valuable to the organization, he does not have much chance of getting ahead. However, a supervisor is perceived as an active contributor occupying an important post, so his name will often be proposed when candidates are considered for a new job. These notions received some support in a study by Grusky (1960), who observed which positions on a baseball team had been played by men who eventually became team managers. He reported that catchers were most often chosen to run a club. Grusky's explanation is that catchers physically face all the rest of the team during a game, direct the team's defensive maneuvers, tell the pitcher what to throw, and in other ways have more influence on teammates than do other players. The catchers' role, in short, allows them to rehearse being a manager.

Hypothesis: An associate, in contrast to a supervisor, is seldom a source of threat to colleagues.

An individual is a threat to others if he causes them to think he will inflict evil or damage on them. An associate will not often be viewed as such a misuser of his power because he works with ideas and does not have the means to put the ideas into force; others must do that. A supervisor, however, controls the fates of subordinates and thus is more likely to be seen as a potential or actual threat to his subordinates.

Hypothesis: A manager evaluates the work of his own associate in terms of its value to himself but evaluates the work of a supervisor in terms of how well the supervisor's department performs.

An associate's job is to help the manager, so the manager will judge the quality of his aide's efforts according to the quality and quantity of help the latter has provided him. A supervisor, in contrast, must help his department. The standards of excellence his unit must achieve are precisely stated, so it is easy for him to observe whether his unit has met them or not. A supervisor's own records and the output of his unit then can make him somewhat immune to the evaluations of his boss, but not completely.

In light of the assumptions about associates and supervisors and the contrasting relationship that associates and supervisors have with their colleagues, we anticipate that occupants of these two posts will develop contrasting views of themselves. An associate gives advice, makes a report, and answers questions, but he has no obligation to follow through on his words; after he delivers them he usually can forget them. The associate's major satisfaction, accordingly, comes from efforts in planning, problem solving, or making policy. He seldom follows through, in fact, because he seldom is asked to implement his beliefs, and therefore he cannot attain satisfaction from such efforts. The supervisor is in a situation unlike that of the associate. He knows exactly what he and his unit must accomplish and he holds himself responsible for the completion of those goals.

Hypothesis: An associate, compared to a supervisor, is less likely to exaggerate his own importance.

An associate will seldom have the kind of experience a supervisor meets every day as he responds to apple polishers, handles a stressful crisis, makes a speech, or in other ways is made to feel that he is an important person. Because the associate has little impact on his colleagues, he cannot easily develop a too grandiose notion about his ability as a leader or influential official.

Hypothesis: An associate, compared to a supervisor, will evaluate his work more favorably.

An associate develops a favorable self-regard because he does not know any better. His job is ambiguous, and achievement in it is difficult to evaluate. He seldom gets much feedback about whether he has succeeded or failed, and, in accord with the rule that no news is good news (Zander, 1971), he tends to assume he has done well. Evaluative comments made by the manager about the associate are more likely to be favorable than unfavorable because the aide's role exists to help the boss. If that help is not forthcoming, if the boss does not approve of his associate's work, he can transfer the latter elsewhere. As long as a given person is in an associate's job, he will probably be approved by his boss, and this appraisal will reach the associate.

On the other hand, a supervisor will less often feel happy about his own work. As noted, any discrepancy between the standard of excellence for his group and the group's actual output can be neatly stated. His unit will fail to attain this criterion part of the time, so he cannot develop an enduring feeling of success. Other demands made of the supervisor are also goal-like in nature, and his failure to attain the demands may be widely visible. It may be easier to feel good about oneself in an ambiguous job (associate) than in a well-defined one (supervisor).

Hypothesis: An associate is not as fearful of making an error as a supervisor is.

Because an associate will respect his own efforts, he is unlikely to be sensitive to the unfavorable consequences of failure. And because the manager approves of his activities, the associate will not dread the reaction of the boss should he make a mistake. Also, the associate need not fear retribution from his colleagues if he errs because news of his boner will probably not reach far. A supervisor, however, cannot ignore what might happen if he commits an error.

Hypothesis: An associate likes his job better than a supervisor does.

The rewards are easier to obtain, with less confusion or strain, in the associate's role than in the supervisor's. Thus the former job should be more attractive than the latter, provided, of course, that the rewards are prized by the associate.

The separate positions of associate and supervisor require the occupants to have different kinds of skills. These skills are either brought to the job or developed while at work.

Hypothesis: An associate will be stronger in technical skills than in administrative or human relations skills. A supervisor will be stronger in administrative and human relations skills than in technical skills.

An associate must be an expert, a technically skilled person, in several senses. In the issues he is asked to study or solve he must be able, and he must display some expertise if he is to be persuasive in his reports to his boss. If he does not have the knowledge he needs when he begins work on an assignment, the associate becomes an expert on that issue by the time he finishes it. Plainly his usefulness depends on his informed competence. A supervisor, in contrast, is expected to deal with technical matters as necessary, but his prime contribution will be through his ability to act as an administrator and to work well with subordinates, to the end that his unit accomplishes its goals.

Hypothesis: An associate will be less ambitious than a supervisor.

Any individual who accepts the job of associate must be self-effacing to some degree or must learn to be that way. He will not obtain much fulfillment of a lust for power because the role of associate offers few opportunities for such gratification. And the occupant of this job will have little need for achievement, or he must satisfy a strong need in ways that do not depend on upward mobility. For example, often an associate is a veteran whose contribution in this post is intellectually satisfying to him because he draws on his experience and knowledge in solving complex problems. A supervisor's job provides a different set of stimuli; his experiences at work, his successes, and his growth all foster and encourage a desire to get ahead in the organization.

Hypothesis: An associate will have better health than a supervisor.

The associate experiences less stress, develops less sense of strain, and moves at a slower pace than the supervisor does. As a result, he will maintain better health and will more consistently avoid illness caused by a hectic pace than a supervisor will.

Summary

There are interesting differences in the work-styles of two kinds of managers called associates and supervisors. Three of the most obvious contrasts, assuming that the occupants of these two roles are similar in status and salary, are: an associate has (compared to a supervisor) a less precisely defined set of duties, a smaller proportion of interactions with subordinates than with the boss, and more responsibilities toward the boss than toward the organization. Because of these differences in their roles, the persons who occupy these separate posts will be dissimilar in their relationships with persons in the rest of the organization, their superior, their responses to their experiences, and the personal qualities they bring to their jobs.

Chapter Nine

Coping with New Regulations

These days, when people in almost any occupation gather at a convention they inevitably talk a good deal about the inconvenience created by another new law. Business people in regulated fields like airlines, pharmaceuticals, or utilities complain with feeling (and practice) about the increasing constraints they must endure. Officers in other businesses are equally loud, and their remarks are echoed by hospital managers, church group leaders, university administrators, city mayors, union bosses, and others. All agree that yearly an additional crust of rules and regulations is pressed on their organization and that each new prod or constraint requires some kind of change within their units. Administrators must be flexible planners and organizers if they are to help their institutions respond appropriately to such external pressures without creating a minor rebellion among their colleagues.

The content of the new regulations is familiar in some cases but brand new in others. Among the emphases in commonly regulated activities are rules about food handling, facilities for the handicapped, noise, dirty air, drugs on the market, and medical care. There are new regulations about taxes, insurance, pension funds, employment compensation, social security, patents, trade secrets, and how individuals are to be treated, disciplined, taught, selected, judged, or given opportunities for certain positions or privileges. Additional rules limit information and its access, concealment, and classification. Finally, a host of most modern constraints restrict freedom of research by regulating the proper care of persons who may be subjects of study, the use of animals in medical investigations, work with recombinant DNA, studies of viruses, work with carcinogens, use of radioactive materials in therapy or research, and others. Most of these rules originate in Washington, D.C., but they also can be the product of a state's or city's legislative body and professional associations. How do organizations respond to these rules? There has been no study of that question. And there has been no investigation of the varied effects regulations can have on an organization. There has been some observation of how parts of an organization's environment can influence the output or procedures within it; those who write about these matters are students of business firms who believe that aspects of a company's surroundings, such as customers, fashions, available resources, and the like, are determinants of its health and wealth (Emery and Trist, 1965; Lawrence and Lorsch, 1967). Shortell (1977) attempted to identify general properties of any kind of organization. Other scholars have been interested in the certainty, predictability, or changeability of the environment in such properties as sociotechnology, the talents and interests of members, or the diversity of critical qualities in the surroundings.

These commentators have limited their attention to features

of the environment that modify an organization's efforts to produce. The scholars have not studied what is of interest to us: the new regulations that arise outside a group and thus influence events inside the group. These rules can either introduce valued new behavior or restrict and prevent unwanted behavior among members. Without wishing to do so, an organization subject to such rules often must develop a policing unit to enforce internal rules that have been prepared by external agents. Let us consider what special problems arise within an organization as it develops ways of controlling its members.

Origins of Regulations

Laws for the control of organizations are appearing at an accelerating rate. This was not always the case; many years ago all laws concerned only the behavior of individuals rather than organizations because organizations (especially corporations) were considered legal fictions "with no pants to kick or soul to damn." Actions could not be attributed to organizations, only to individuals, and therefore a group as such could not obey or break a law. And a group's members could not be held responsible for activities in behalf of the corporation because their liability was limited to specific things they had been told to do as employees—and no one was ever told, of course, to break a law. But by 1860, according to Stone (1975), corporations could no longer be ignored as wrongdoers; railroad firms and other types of businesses were engaging in injurious practices that had to be restricted. Nowadays, as we remarked, there are all kinds of laws for all kinds of organizations.

The general purposes of these regulations are to either spread losses so that these are fairly shared or eliminate activities that damage others' welfare or rights. In recent years the things considered to be losses of rights or harmful have increased in number and kind. A larger legal tent covers more and more organizational action. Why?

For one thing, there has been an increasing demand for accountability, meaning that those who spend taxpayers' money or who charge customers for services or products are being watched more closely to see that they provide what they are paid to provide. To some degree the cause for the increased interest in accountability is based on a distrust of organizations by lawmakers and consumers. Joseph Califano, the new secretary of the Department of Health, Education and Welfare, recognized this mood in February 1977 when he told a group of university officials that he was concerned about the present approach to regulations "which assumes that everyone will violate the law." An educator at the same meeting deplored what he termed the "obsession of the HEW with fraud and abuse." The lively interest in rules to protect health and welfare also stems from increasing uneasiness about modern forms of technology, which arouse desires for protection against new products or processes. Unusual ideas are often a source of fear, and legislative bodies accordingly may try to control statements of belief in sexual, political, religious, or other matters. Many modern regulations are to support the civil rights of individuals who have been disadvantaged. Laws, it is assumed, can generate improved conditions for these persons.

Effects of Regulations

Most organizations comply with new regulations more often than not. Nevertheless, members frequently make efforts to prevent implementation of the law or to change parts of it in some way. There are a number of things they can do. A common maneuver is to declare that the legislation does not "apply to us." They try to establish that their organization is not to be covered because it is constitutionally autonomous, tax exempt, not engaged in interstate commerce, or excluded on some other grounds. A law may be interpreted so that it does not cover this organization or many parts of it; thus a rule requiring all meetings within an organization to be open to the public might be viewed as fitting the top decision-making body in the organization, but no other part.

A different form of resistance attempts to get the regulation changed through letters to legislators, oral appeals to them by lobbyists, or testimonials at congressional hearings. A number of units may join hands, through a national association, to create public pressure toward change. The content of the law may be studied to determine whether its wording adequately conforms to the original intent of the legislation. An organization (unlike an individual) may claim "limited liability," meaning that the regulation is to cover only a limited proportion of the members, while they are doing a limited number of things. A less savory form of resistance is in use when officers cover up wrongdoing and thereby avoid the impact of the regulation. In his 1975 book, *Where the Law Ends,* Stone described how many employees of an insurance company cheerfully broke the law by writing fake insurance policies so that it appeared the firm had had more income than it actually had earned, thereby avoiding the effect of bankruptcy regulations.

What conditions cause an organization to resist a new rule rather than wholeheartedly comply with it? There are no studies of that question I know about, but it is possible to make some guesses. Generally speaking, if compliance, rather than resistance, will generate more repulsive consequences, the members are more likely to drag their feet or actively resist. These repulsive consequences stem from either the content or the method of the regulation. The law's content, what it requires or forbids, will stimulate resistance if members believe that the new rule is not really needed in their unit or that the results from complying with it will be less satisfactory than practices currently followed there. The method of the regulation, which is the way the rule is presented to the target groups or the way it attempts to obtain adherence to the rule, will be a source of resistance if the rule is seen to be capricious, arbitrary, amateurish, or ill advised. Also, a rule may be resisted if it is petty in detail, technically inaccurate, incomprehensible, inconsistent within itself, or constantly being changed. A regulation is not happily accepted if it demands excessive work in completing forms, obtaining data, training staff members, revising equipment, or keeping records. It may be met with resistance if the rule is not enforced, no matter how often it is broken, or if it cannot be enforced because transgressions of the rule are not detectable. And a law is not likely to be respected if the sanctions on those who break it are too weak to worry about or too small to do any harm. A large corporation can afford to pay a fine (even a large one) if doing so does not require it to stop illegal (profitable) actions. No doubt resistance is stronger in some situations than in others, as is suggested in the following assumption.

Assumption: The strength of an organization's resistance to a new regulation depends on the degree of incompatibility between the new rule and current practices in the organization as well as on the amount of value members place on their current practices.

An example of incompatibility between a new rule and an old practice is the difference between a newly mandated regulation requiring physicians on the staff of a hospital to appraise one another's methods of treatment, on the one hand, and the preexisting rule in which the work quality of each doctor had never been appraised by anyone, on the other hand. Another example is the introduction of cross-district bussing of schoolchildren instead of previous within-district bussing. Rules for providing equal opportunity in hiring create incompatibility for some kinds of institutions and none at all for others, depending on their procedures in these matters. A worldwide example of resistance when a past practice was replaced by a new requirement is the controversy within the Catholic church between those who wish mass to be said in Latin (the preexisting practice) and those who require that it be said in the language of the nation where the mass is being held. All in all, there may be more resistance to a new rule as the decision makers in the organization are more certain of the importance of their current practice and are more committed to it. Generally, the strength of this resistance will be only great enough to prevent compliance with the undesirable parts of a new regulation.

The organization's officers will more completely *comply* with a new piece of legislation, rather than resist it, if doing so will generate more favorable consequences or fewer repulsive acts. As before, these desirable results are affected by the content or method of the rule. The content of a rule will stimulate compliance if it might produce more favorable results for the organization than current procedures do. As an illustration, in accordance with modern building codes, an organization may make expensive changes in physical facilities that will benefit handicapped persons (ramps, low curbs, larger stalls for toilets) because its officers believe these changes are needed in their building and the regulations now justify the expense.

The way a law is developed and made known to organizations—the method of the law—also has a great deal to do with the willingness of these agencies to accept rather than resist it. Compliance will be more likely to occur if the need for a regulation was originally suggested by those it is to govern and even more likely if the wording of the rule is planned by such persons. The way is also smoothed for compliance if first drafts of legislation are made available for comments by those who will be targets of the law. It is also true, in contrast, that the punishments members of an organization will endure if they do not abide by the rule encourage members to comply. The size of a fine that a guilty group will be required to pay or the length of a sentence in jail for certain officers, the loss of a license, or the loss of other privileges are sanctions that can seldom be ignored. It is an important research topic to determine whether compliance to a regulation is greater (more complete) when units under a regulation had some say in developing it, or whether compliance is greater if the costs for failing to comply are stricter. Our guess is that each—participation and sanction—are effective in obtaining compliance. Where one of these stimulants to compliance is effectively operating, however, the other cannot function. Probably the side effects of participation are more healthy for the organization (positive acceptance) than the side effects of obeying a rule merely in order to avoid punishments (resentment). The degree of compliance will be greater if the rule is more useful to the organization, a notion employed in the next assumption.

Assumption: The strength of compliance to a new regulation depends on the degree of compatibility between the content or method of the rule and current practices or beliefs in the organization as well as on the amount of value members place on the requirements of the new rule.

In accord with this assumption an organization is more likely to comply with a rule when decision makers more strongly believe it promises a better way to achieve important ends than was being used before the rule.

Other matters affect how strongly members accept a regulation or resist it. One such matter is the social reaction, for or against the rule, that arises outside the organization. There have been subgroups composed of critics or advocates recently because of regulations on the use of certain medicines, guidelines for research on recombinant DNA, laws for hiring handicapped persons, and proliferation of power plants. Such social action groups deepen the understanding (pro and con) of officials and members as they evaluate a controversial regulation. A law with an impact on all parts of an organization is perhaps more conducive to stronger resistance or compliance than one that affects only a few departments or persons.

Enforcing a Regulation

When decision makers are faced with a new regulation and decide not to resist it, they must plan how they will implement it, to whom the law applies within the organization, what these persons must do to comply with the rule, how they can be helped to do those things, and how their degree of adherence can be monitored. In some cases the planning process is rather casual; in other cases the plans are laid with great care.

Assumption: As an organization's decision makers more strongly accept a regulation they invest more resources in planning how to implement the regulation.

The decision makers must figure out how much they ought to invest in preparing plans. The simplest procedure, requiring the least resources, is to announce its existence while requesting that each member behave appropriately. Examples are a new law about income taxes, a new requirement for protection against fire, or a new set of guidelines for disposing of hazardous materials. This relaxed approach is more likely to be used when a member's deviation from the law is her own fault, not that of the organization;

when any deviant action is easy to detect; when sanctions against deviation are minor for individual or group; and when members welcome the rule and need only be reminded about it, not pressed to obey it.

In planning that asks for somewhat deeper involvement, members' suggestions are solicited in meetings, by letters, or by a more sophisticated survey method. This procedure is most useful when members would benefit from suggestions by their peers about how each of them might behave.

Still greater investment of the organization's personnel, energy, time, or funds is exemplified by the appointment of a committee to think about how the rule will affect the organization, how it should be enforced, how special precautions should be arranged, and so on. The idea is that a uniform policy or plan is needed for all parts of the organization. This process is used when deviation by members must be prevented because the institution as a whole would be liable, the sanctions for breaking the law are serious, and the rule needs careful study so its implications for the organization are clearly identified. Usually such a committee reports its recommendations to some executive or body who settles upon the final plan. It is common these days to have several such planning groups, each representing some special interest within the organization.

A more extreme drain upon an organization's resources occurs when regular employees are assigned the full-time task of developing a plan. Usually these employees are experts who can do this well but who must neglect their regular duties to make the plan. These experts may use any or all of the procedures already mentioned, but they are responsible for coming up with a proposal that will be efficient and will ensure that the organization and its parts abide by the new rule.

Some new laws are relevant only to particular departments within a large agency or to sets of specialists who do the things that are touched by the rules. For example, regulations about handling of foods, use of benzine, access to unemployment insurance, or disposal of waste will be more salient to some members than to others. When a regulation has a specific target, planning for adherence is simpler and less costly for the larger organization. Once a plan of action is proposed, it must be appraised and approved (or rejected) by officials who have the authority to do so. Because the top officers in any unit are more vulnerable to social pressures, often persons who oppose a plan will loudly claim the plan is wrong so that the superior decision makers in the organization must attend to the matter. That group of superiors can then be exposed to social pressures as it decides how it will respond to the rule.

Control Methods

To enforce a new rule, administrative procedures must be put in place, and particular persons must be asked to take care of these. We assume that the degree of investment in such matters is also governed by the acceptance of the regulation.

Assumption: As an organization's decision makers more strongly accept a regulation, they invest more resources in enforcing the regulation.

There are five main ways a rule can be enforced:

1. Posting a notice. The rule is made public under the belief that this is enough to ensure conformity.
2. Creating a monitoring committee. A group of employees meet now and then to make sure that actions by parts of the organization conform to the rule. Such a committee may have the right to approve or disapprove plans for actions to be governed by the law. The committee might also examine machinery, equipment, or operations conducted within a department. Such a committee will be more effective if the events it controls occur infrequently and are easy to detect.
3. Adding the enforcing duty to the job of a person who can readily perform it. This procedure is likely to be used when enforcement is not a heavy task, the enforcer is experienced in the matters to be controlled, and quick action may be necessary. Two examples are an ombudsman who has the right to obtain information from protected files and an affirmative action officer who inspects the compliance of an organization to standards for equal opportunity.

4. Creating a new position and having its occupant work full time to make sure the regulation is followed. This person might watch over methods for protecting individuals against carcinogens, for perfecting ways of obtaining health insurance, or for supervising uses of unusual chemicals. Clearly this kind of post needs an expert and is an expensive addition to an organization.
5. Installing a new officer with a staff that monitors adherence to regulations concerning matters like the sanitary nature or safety of a product, control of pollution, and taxes. Such a group will cost even more than the group in method 4.

A prime problem is how to obtain compliance to a new regulation without planting seeds of internal resistance. Plainly, resistance is less likely to occur if those the rule is to govern are given some say in planning adherence to it, provided they come up with a plan that is worthy of their own support. Many field experiments have shown that decisions by groups tend to generate among members conformity to those decisions (Cartwright and Zander, 1968b). When a regulation is imposed upon an organization, however, there may be little room for such freedom of choice.

We are all familiar with the rules and new regulations that govern the safety or effectiveness of a product and protect us from inadequate drugs, appliances, vehicles, building materials, clothing, and so on. Laws concerned with processes or procedures are less well known but are increasing in number as it has become evident to lawmakers that behavior (and sometimes products) can best be controlled through requiring adherence to certain practices. Such a law does not tell persons in an organization what they must do, but how they must do it. For example, members are not told how many women they must hire; instead they must provide evidence that they have given women an opportunity (equal to that given males) to qualify for an open position. Or, such a law will not specify what must be done with certain wastes; it instead asks officers to demonstrate that they have noted specific standards before disposing of the material. It seems clear that these rules about processes allow room for the judgment needed on technical matters and recognize that pressing for a correct choice at the outset may be more important than controlling a final product when protecting health, welfare, or rights through legislation.

There is reason to believe that regulations concerned with product may be more stringent than those concerned with process because a regulation about a product will concentrate upon its efficacy (does it work?), its side effects (what kind of harm can it cause?), and its safety (how often will these adverse effects occur?). These matters are probably easier to measure and more likely to arouse concern of organizational members than mere adherence to an approved procedure.

Summary

Increasingly, new regulations are pressed on organizations by external agencies and these rules require changes in the affected units. Members of a given organization may make an attempt to prevent implementation of the law, or to revise it in some way, if its content or method is incompatible with preexisting and preferred practices in the group. Members accept a new regulation when it is compatible with and more valued than present behavior. New rules require that plans be made for enforcement of them within that unit and that procedures be activated to ensure that the rules are obeyed. The more that new rules are accepted, the more resources the organization puts into planning and enforcing the regulation.

Chapter Ten

Harmony in Work Groups

In a committee meeting the other day I realized that I was having a good time, the meeting was a pleasant occasion, and others around the table apparently felt the same. The talk was quick and pointed, and differing views arose because problems were being solved, not because intellectual turf was being stubbornly defended. There was good humor, but work was being done.

A bureaucrat is supposed to be bored in a committee meeting. Why was this session a pleasant one? The unit's purpose had much to do with it. The committee was created to respond to a complaint, made by a union of student employees, that giving scholarships to members of minority groups is a form of discrimination against the minorities because recipients of these awards do not have to work for their money and therefore do not engage in teaching or research, a deprivation which limits their intellectual growth. And since the minority scholars are not employees, they are not allowed to join the student union. The union's complaint demanded a serviceable response from the committee, a response that would properly recognize the logic of the complaint and withstand an attack by the union.

There were three other reasons, beyond the nature of the committee's task, that caused members to work well together. Some of the participants were friends. The members had to move quickly because of the impatience of the union. And the committee members were sensitive to the need for effective and harmonious relations in their meetings; this sensitivity aroused loyalty to the group and a desire for a good report by the committee. This meeting was not an isolated event: most people who work in an organization enjoy making things go well and get satisfaction from developing a sound plan. For example, frequently, when a meeting room door opens after a committee has completed a session, the chatter and comments are lively and members say they are delighted with their product. Yet the sources of such cheer are seldom studied. *Joi de group* is commonly thought to be a minor side effect that does not warrant examination, even though it often is the most striking feature of a working unit, especially a face-to-face committee. Thus, in this chapter we shall discuss the origins of group harmony, a condition conducive to members' comfort in relationships with one another.

Assumption: Members of a group are more disposed to encourage a state of group harmony than a state of disharmony.

Efforts to create unpleasantness in a meeting occur but rarely; more often members do whatever is necessary to foster harmony. There is empirical support for this assumption, based on observations of conference groups in military, industry, and community settings (Bales, 1954). Bales noted and coded the interpersonal meaning of each comment made in a meeting. After summarizing these results he reported that members usually reveal twice as many positive reactions (agreement, effort to cause a release of tension, or friendliness) as negative reactions (disagreement, tense behavior, unfriendliness), and this ratio was more typical of more effective groups. In laboratory research, as yet unpublished, Zander noted the number of mutually supportive actions such as praising, approving, agreeing, or helping one another as well as the number of nonsupportive actions such as blaming, derogating, disagreeing, and aggressing among members. He observed more supportive acts than nonsupportive ones while these groups were working on a motor task that required close collaboration; this ratio was stronger in successful groups than in failing ones.

Assumption: A state of group harmony is stronger as the agreement among members on motives is greater.

If group members agree on such components as the intentions of individual members and the group's standards and the members accept these intentions and standards, there will be a state of harmony. Three hypotheses suggest how such harmony might be increased.

Hypothesis: Harmony may be increased among members when each member perceives that other members will accept his intentions and actions.

A variety of things can be done within a group to help each member recognize that his wishes and moves may be accepted, or at least not rejected, by associates. One method is to select recruits who are similar to a group's current members. Scott (1965) showed that fraternities and sororities prefer joiners whose ideas match those of the members because commonality of belief preserves loyalty and pleasant interpersonal relations. The membership rosters of newly created working committees likewise are often assembled on the basis of who might work well with whom. And ability to get along with others is more important than talent or productivity in determining which scholars are hired for teaching positions in colleges, according to Lewis (1975).

Harmony may be facilitated by encouraging participants to

cling to personal motives that are relevant to colleagues' purposes and to drop motives that are not. Most commonly, such displacement of objectives is accomplished when a member is recruited and learns, during a period of orientation, that some things he hopes to obtain in that group are not obtainable because the group will not tolerate them. In other cases, members may be trained to want things that are acceptable to others. A sense of oneness in purpose among members can also be aroused by generating a single emotional response. For example, the arousers may use humor or invoke enthusiasm, grief, religious awe, fear, or patriotic fervor by such methods as a brass band, singing, or cheering.

If members can earn individual rewards in a group when they qualify for the rewards, a manager may encourage consonance by promising that she will equitably distribute the gains. And to make the group members feel she will fairly distribute the personal rewards, the manager can establish a group goal and a mutual interdependence among members—they will then see that a gain by one is a gain by all or that a loss by one is a loss by all. A group incentive plan, in which all members share alike in rewards earned by the group, is an apt illustration of this procedure. In such a cooperative unit members readily recognize the legitimacy of one another's needs, develop support for each other, and accept values that are suited to such behavior (Deutsch, 1973). Also, in a cooperative group members help one another (more than in a noncooperative group), which suggests that each member accepts the others' intentions and actions.

Hypothesis: Harmony may be increased among members as each member conforms to social pressures directed toward support of the unit's standards.

As we all know, groups can and often do put pressures on their members to bring about a uniformity of beliefs, attitudes, values, and behavior. The uniformity being sought in such instances is an adherence to a group standard, a more or less conscious agreement about matters of mutual interest to separate members or to the group as a whole. Once a standard has been established, members tend to protect it by pressing one another to adhere to its requirements. The result of such pressures, if they are effective, is consonance in the intentions and actions of participants.

Clearly, it takes some degree of harmony to invent a viable and potent group standard. It also takes some degree of harmony for each participant to be willing to place pressure on others and to accept pressure toward adhering to the standard. For example, it is known that the power of a group over its members is a function of the cohesiveness of the group. Cohesiveness, in this instance, is the desire among members to remain members (Cartwright and Zander, 1968b). We cannot say which comes first, group harmony or group standard, but each is necessary if there is to be consonance in a group.

Those who make decisions for a group want to ensure that the group has enough power to determine the intentions and actions of its members. One way this can be done is to establish that the group has the right to require particular behavior and that members have the duty to obey these requirements. If a group is part of a larger organization, such legitimacy may be developed in the smaller unit when it is first created by having officials in the bigger unit assign individuals to the smaller group. By giving a group a name and a purpose, the officials imply that it has a legitimate status; this legitimacy of social power can be created by the initial members as they establish rights and duties for themselves.

A way to strengthen the power of a group is to increase members' commitment to the group. Some organizations work hard to foster this commitment. Kanter (1972) described practices communes used to tie the participants to them: sacrifice for the commune, investment in it, communion among members, or mortification of the self. Occasionally it is necessary to convince a member (especially one whose loyalty to the group is wavering) that he needs the group by urging him to recognize that the advantages he derives from membership cannot be found elsewhere. And sometimes it is necessary to determine what a member wants from a membership and to explain to him how this will be fulfilled by his group. We need more, better controlled studies of the ways in which commitment to a group can be aroused and a better understanding of how these methods work.

Acceptable group influence can be generated by creating an illusion of unity among persons, by helping members recognize that they make up a single entity. This can be accomplished by placing members in proximity to one another, as in a military platoon or in common living quarters, by addressing them as members of that unit, by asking them to choose a name for their group, and by helping them see that all members are moving in the same direction at the same time (Zander, Stotland, and Wolfe, 1960). Groups with greater unity should have a stronger influence on the beliefs of members and be more attractive to members.

Hypothesis: Harmony may be increased among members by developing a stronger desire for achievement of group success.

The desire for group achievement is a disposition of members to develop pride in their group's accomplishments. When this desire is stronger, a group is more productive and the members work together better because each participant seeks an end that is also being sought by groupmates. The desire for group success increases in strength as the group is more successful. Thus a measure that generates more of this desire creates more harmony within a group.

Assumption: Members' efforts to reduce disharmony in a group are stronger as the disharmony is greater.

Disharmony increases as there is less consonance among the intentions and actions of members. This lack of consonance within a group is evident when there are unresolvable differences among members, unwillingness among them to engage in a joint task or to persist in it, formation of rivalrous groups, resignations from the group, refusal of members to accept assignments, rejection of the organization's officials, or derogation of the group and its work. Disharmony also has effects upon individuals: anxiety, ineffective participation, psychosomatic disorders, and undue hostility, among other results.

Assumption: Members become more tolerant of group disharmony when it is necessary for the good of the group.

Writers about group management often describe the value of conflict within a group, the cleansing quality of a good argument, the commitment that grows out of a settled quarrel, and so on (Deutsch, 1973). And indeed, under certain circumstances disharmony may be tolerated by group members if it is a side effect of an event that itself is valued. For example, a tough critique of a platoon by a drill sergeant, a scolding of a team by an athletic coach, or an unfavorable appraisal of a group by its own members may arouse an unpleasant tension, but this tension will be endured if the members believe that the development of better practices can follow from awareness of the group's inadequacies. The work an individual is asked to perform within an organization may not be what she prefers to do, and so this duty itself may be a source of disharmony. If the person's assignment is important for the success of the group, however, she is more certain to do in good grace whatever is needed. Most likely this inclination will be stronger as her desire for group success is greater. As other examples, disharmony is acceptable to participants in group therapy, marriage counseling, labor-management negotiations, and organizations that are making changes or displacing a leader because such situations stimulate improvements or are intended to do so.

Our guess is that disharmony is more tolerable if it is created by the actions of persons outside the group rather than by those inside it. As discussed in Chapter 4, external agents can have an influence on a group's plans and thus on the amount of consonance among members because most groups (other than those devoted to teaching or therapy) exist to provide a service to people in the group's environment. These people may be customers, rivals, superiors, subordinates, or dependents; they have a right to make demands on the group, even unpleasant ones.

Events within a group may be less harmonious for some members than for others. In such an instance, efforts to reduce this unpleasantness probably will be directed toward relieving the persons who are more uncomfortable. But such efforts may not be made if the uncomfortable member is unattractive to the remaining participants. (A member is unattractive to his colleagues if the members place low value on his acts or attributes and if they feel he will often act that way within the group.) We therefore expect that disharmony in a group will occur more often for attractive members than for unattractive ones.

Groups at Work

Within any organization some persons are better qualified to reduce disharmony. A superior in a hierarchical system, for example, can lower unpleasantness more effectively than can his subordinates. Subordinates may in fact realize that they do not have enough influence to generate a change and thus make no efforts to change things because their efforts may only generate conflict and not improve matters. We thus anticipate that superiors, compared to subordinates, will make more attempts, and successful ones, to achieve harmony in a group.

The nature of some social roles requires a person to help develop harmony, such as jobs in which individuals like salespeople, legislators, waiters, repairmen, or nurses must serve others. Some people—ministers, psychotherapists, teachers, or personnel managers—have to be supportive of others. And some people, like negotiators for labor-management conflicts, referees, and judges, direct their efforts toward reducing differences among the intentions of colleagues. Clearly, many persons in our society are expected to be sensitive to the presence of disharmony in interpersonal relationships and to do something about them.

Summary

Sometimes the harmony among members is the outstanding feature of a work group. Members usually are more disposed to encourage group harmony than disharmony and thus they foster it by generating greater consonance between the motives of members and the goals of their group. Disharmony is acceptable in a group when it occurs as a by-product of events that are otherwise good for the group.

References

ANDERSON, W. A. *Some Participation Principles, Their Relations to the Programs of Rural Agencies.* Ithaca, N.Y.: Cornell University Extension Bulletin, 1947.

ARONSON, E., and MILLS, T. "Effect of Severity of Initiation on Liking for a Group." *Journal of Abnormal and Social Psychology,* 1959, *59,* 177–181.

BALES, R. F. "In Conference." *Harvard Business Review,* 1954, *32,* 44–50.

BLAKE, R., MOUTON, J., and SLOMA, R. "The Union-Management Intergroup Laboratory." *Journal of Applied Behavioral Science,* 1965, *1,* 25–57.

BLANCHARD, A., ADELMAN, L., and COOK, S. "Effects of Group Success and Failure upon Interpersonal Attraction in Cooperating Interracial Groups." *Journal of Personality and Social Psychology,* 1975, *31,* 1020–1030.

BOWERS, D., and SEASHORE, S. "Predicting Organizational Effectiveness with a Four-Factor Theory of Leadership." *Administrative Science Quarterly,* 1966, *11,* 238–263.

BOWMAN, G. *The Image of the Promotable Person in Business Enterprise.* Ann Arbor, Mich.: University Microfilms, 1962.

CAPLOW, T., and MC GEE, R. J. *The Academic Marketplace.* New York: Basic Books, 1958.

CARTWRIGHT, D. "The Nature of Group Cohesiveness." In D. Cartwright and A. Zander (Eds.), *Group Dynamics Research and Theory.* New York: Harper & Row, 1968.

CARTWRIGHT, D., and ZANDER, A. *Group Dynamics Research and Theory.* New York: Harper & Row, 1968a.

CARTWRIGHT, D., and ZANDER, A. "Pressures to Uniformity in Groups." In D. Cartwright and A. Zander (Eds.), *Group Dynamics Research and Theory.* New York: Harper & Row, 1968b.

CHEVALIER, M., BAILEY, M., and BURNS, T. "Toward a Framework for Large-Scale Problem Management." *Human Relations,* 1975, *27,* 43–69.

CHU, G. C., RAHIM, S. A., and KINCAID, D. L. *Communication for Group Transformation in Development.* Honolulu, Hawaii: East-West Center, 1976.

CLARK, B. R. "The 'Cooling Out' Function in Higher Education." *American Journal of Sociology,* 1960, *65,* 569–576.

COOK, D. *Program Evaluation and Review Technique: Application in Education.* Cooperative Research Monograph 17. Washington, D.C.: United States Office of Education, 1966.

COULTER, F., and TAFT, R. "The Professional Assimilation of Schoolteachers as Social Assimilation." *Human Relations,* 1973, *26,* 681–693.

CULLITON, B. "Freedom of Information Can Work." *Science,* 1975a, *188,* 812.

CULLITON, B. "NSF: Defense of Closed Peer Review System Not Persuasive." *Science,* 1975b, *189,* 535–537.

References

DELBECA, A., and VAN DE VEN, A. "A Group Process Model for Problem Identification and Program Planning." *Journal of Applied Behavioral Science,* 1971, *7,* 466–492.

DELBECA, A., VAN DE VEN, A., and GUSTAFSON, D. *Group Techniques for Program Planning.* Glenview, Ill.: Scott, Foresman, 1975.

DENNY, B. C. "The Decline of Merit." *Science,* 1974, *186,* 875.

DERBYSHIRE, R. C. "Medical Ethics and Discipline." *Journal of American Medical Association,* 1974, *228,* 59–62.

DEUTSCH, M. "The Effects of Cooperation and Competition upon Group Process." *Human Relations,* 1949, *2,* 129–152 and 199–231.

DEUTSCH, M. *The Resolution of Conflict.* New Haven, Conn.: Yale University Press, 1973.

DOWLING, H. F. *Medicines for Man.* New York: Knopf, 1973.

EMERSON, R. "Mount Everest: A Case Study of Communication Feedback and Sustained Goal Striving." *Sociometry,* 1966, *29,* 213–277.

EMERY, F. E., and TRIST, E. "The Causal Texture of Organizational Environments." *Human Relations,* 1965, *18,* 21–32.

ETZIONI, A. *Modern Organizations.* Englewood Cliffs, N.J.: Prentice-Hall, 1964.

ETZIONI, A. "An Engineer-Social Science Team at Work." *Massachusetts Institute of Technology Review,* 1975, *25,* 27–31.

FERGUSON, C., and KELLEY, H. "Significant Factors in Overevaluation of Own-Group's Product." *Journal of Abnormal and Social Psychology,* 1964, *69,* 223–227.

FESTINGER, L. "Informal Social Communication." *Psychological Review,* 1950, *57,* 271–282.

FESTINGER, L., RIECKEN, H., and SCHACHTER, S. *When Prophecy Fails.* Minneapolis: University of Minnesota Press, 1956.

FESTINGER, L., SCHACHTER, S., and BACK, K. *Social Pressures in Informal Groups.* New York: Harper & Row, 1950.

FORWARD, J. "Group Achievement Motivation and Individual Motives To Achieve Success and To Avoid Failure." *Journal of Personality,* 1969, *37,* 297–309.

FORWARD, J., and ZANDER, A. "Choice of Unattainable Group Goals and Effects on Performance." *Organizational Behavior and Human Performance,* 1971, *6,* 184–199.

FRENCH, J. R. P., and RAVEN, B. "The Bases of Social Power." In D. Cartwright (Ed.), *Studies in Social Power.* Ann Arbor: Institute for Social Research, University of Michigan, 1959.

GARFINKEL, H. "Conditions of Successful Degradation Ceremonies." *American Journal of Sociology,* 1956, *61,* 420–424.

GEORGOPOULOS, B., and MANN, F. *The Community General Hospital.* New York: Macmillan, 1962.

GOFFMAN, E. "On Cooling the Mark Out." *Psychiatry,* 1952, *15,* 451–463.

GROSS, N., MASON, W., and MC EACHERN, A. *Explorations in Role Analysis.* New York: Wiley, 1958.

GRUSKY, O. "Administrative Succession in Formal Organizations." *Social Forces,* 1960, *39,* 105–115.

HALAL, W. E. "Toward a General Theory of Leadership." *Human Relations,* 1974, *27,* 401–416.

HAMBLIN, R. L. "Leadership and Crises." *Sociometry,* 1958, *21,* 322–335.

HAMMOND, K., and ADELMAN, L. "Science, Values, and Human Judgment." *Science,* 1976, *194,* 389–396.

HEPP, T. "Attitudinal Change as the Groundwork for Socio-Economic Development." Unpublished manuscript, provided by author, 1975.

HOFFER, E. *The True Believer.* New York: Harper & Row, 1951.

HOLDEN, C. "Congress Strengthens Freedom of Information Act." *Science,* 1975a, *187,* 242.

HOLDEN, C. "Privacy: Congressional Efforts Are Coming to Fruition." *Science,* 1975b, *188,* 713–715.

HOLLANDER, E. "Competence and Conformity in the Acceptance of Influence." *Journal of Abnormal and Social Psychology,* 1961, *61,* 365–370.

HUENEFELD, J. *The Community Activist's Handbook.* Boston: Beacon Press, 1970.

JACKSON, J. "A Space for Conceptualizing Person-Group Relationships." *Human Relations,* 1959, *12,* 3–15.

JANIS, I. *Victims of Groupthink.* Boston: Houghton Mifflin, 1972.

KANTER, R. *Commitment and Community, Communes and Utopias in Perspective.* Cambridge, Mass.: Harvard University Press, 1972.

KANTROWITZ, A., and others. "The Science Court Experiment, An Interim Report." *Science,* 1976, *193,* 653–656.

KATZ, D. "The Motivational Basis of Organizational Behavior." *Behavioral Science,* 1964, *9,* 131–146.

KELLER, P., and BROWN, C. T. "An Interpersonal Ethic for Communication." In J. M. Civilky (Ed.), *Messages, a Reader in Communication.* New York: Random House, 1974.

KUPPERMAN, R. H., WILCOX, R. H., and SMITH, H. A. "Crisis Management: Some Opportunities." *Science,* 1975, *187,* 404–410.

LAWRENCE, P., and LORSCH, J. W. *Organization and Environment.* Homewood, Ill.: Irwin, 1967.

LEEDES, F. J., and GILBERT, H. J. *Corpus Juris Secondum.* Brooklyn, N.Y.: American Law Book Co., 1961.

LEVI, A., and BENJAMIN, A. "Jews and Arabs Rehearse Geneva: A Model of Conflict Resolution." *Human Relations,* 1976, *29,* 1035–1044.

LEWIS, L. S. *Scaling the Ivory Tower.* Baltimore: Johns Hopkins University Press, 1975.

LIKERT, R. *New Patterns of Management.* New York: McGraw-Hill, 1959.

MC GREGOR, D. *The Human Side of Enterprise.* New York: McGraw-Hill, 1959.

MAIER, N. R. F. *Problem Solving Discussion and Conferences: Leadership Methods and Skills.* New York: McGraw-Hill, 1963.

MEDOW, H., and ZANDER, A. "Aspirations for Group Chosen by Central and Peripheral Members." *Journal of Personality and Social Psychology,* 1965, *1,* 224–228.

MULDER, M., RITESEMA VAN ECK, J., and DE JONG, R. "An Organization in Crisis and Non-crisis Situations." *Human Relations,* 1971, *24,* 19–41.

NADER, R., PETKAS, P., and BLACKWELL, K. *Whistle Blowing.* New York: Bantam Books, 1972.

NEWCOMB, T. *The Acquaintance Process.* New York: Holt, Rinehart and Winston, 1961.

PAINES, R., HENCH, H., and ZINN, K. *A Brief Guide to CONFER II for Computer Based Conferencing.* Ann Arbor: Center for Research on Learning and Teaching, University of Michigan, 1976.

PEPITONE, E. "Responsibility to Group and Its Effects on the Performance of Members." Unpublished doctoral dissertation, University of Michigan, 1952.

QUINN, J., and MAJOR, R. "Norway: Small Country Plans Civil Science Technology." *Science,* 1974, *183,* 172–179.

QUINN, R., TABOR, J., and GORDON, L. *The Decision to Discriminate.* Ann Arbor: Survey Research Center, University of Michigan, 1968.

REDMAN, E. *The Dance of Legislation.* New York: Simon and Schuster, 1973.

"Report of Task Force on Citizen Participation in the United States Department of Health, Education and Welfare." *Federal Register,* 1976, *41,* 49773–49781.

ROSEN, S. "On Reluctance to Communicate Undesirable Information: The MUM Effect." *Sociometry,* 1970, *33,* 253–263.

ROSS, I., and ZANDER, A. "Need Satisfaction and Employee Turnover." *Personnel Psychology,* 1957, *10,* 327–338.

SCHACHTER, S. "Deviation, Rejection, and Communication." *Journal of Abnormal and Social Psychology,* 1951, *46,* 190–207.

SCOTT, W. *Values and Organizations.* Chicago: Rand McNally, 1965.

SHERIDAN, T. B. "Community Dialog Technology." *Proceedings of the International Society of Electrical Engineers,* 1975, *63,* 563–575.

SHORTELL, S. M. "The Role of Environment in a Configurational

Theory of Organizations." *Human Relations,* 1977, *30,* 275–302.

SILLS, D. L. *The Volunteers.* New York: Free Press, 1957.

SLESINGER, J. *Personal Adaptation in the Federal Junior Management Assistant Program.* Michigan Governmental Studies, No. 41. Ann Arbor: Institute of Public Administration, 1961.

SMITH, D. H. "A Psychological Model of Individual Participation in Formal Voluntary Organizations." *American Journal of Sociology,* 1966, *72,* 249–266.

SNOEK, D. "Some Effects of Rejection upon Attraction to a Group." *Journal of Abnormal and Social Psychology,* 1962, *64,* 175–182.

SOLZHENITSYN, A. I. *The Gulag Archipelago.* New York: Harper & Row, 1973.

STONE, C. *Where the Law Ends.* New York: Harper & Row, 1975.

TESSER, A., and ROSEN, S. "The Reluctance To Transmit Bad News." In L. Berkowitz (Ed.), *Advances in Experimental Social Psychology.* New York: Academic Press, 1975.

THOMAS, E. J., and ZANDER, A. "The Relationship of Goal Structure to Motivation Under Extreme Conditions." *Journal of Individual Psychology,* 1959, *15,* 121–127.

TOCH, H. *Social Psychology of Social Movements.* Indianapolis: Bobbs-Merrill, 1965.

VARELO, J. A. *Psychological Solutions to Social Problems.* New York: Academic Press, 1971.

WHYTE, W. K. *Small Groups and Political Rituals in China.* Berkeley: University of California Press, 1974.

WHYTE, W. M. *The Organization Man.* Garden City, N.Y.: Doubleday Anchor, 1956.

ZAND, D. "Trust and Managerial Problem Solving." *Administrative Science Quarterly,* 1972, *17,* 229–239.

ZANDER, A. *Motives and Goals in Groups.* New York: Academic Press, 1971.

ZANDER, A., and ARMSTRONG, W. "Working for Group Pride in a

Slipper Factory." *Journal of Applied Social Psychology,* 1972, *2,* 193–207.

ZANDER, A., and CURTIS, T. "Social Support and Rejection of Organizational Standards." *Journal of Educational Psychology,* 1965, *56,* 87–95.

ZANDER, A., FORWARD, J., and ALBERT, R. "Adaptation of Board Members to Repeated Success and Failure by Their Organizations." *Organizational Behavior and Human Performance,* 1969, *4,* 56–76.

ZANDER, A., FULLER, R., and ARMSTRONG, W. "Attributed Group Pride or Shame in Group or Self." *Journal of Personality and Social Psychology,* 1972, *23,* 346–352.

ZANDER, A., and GYR, J. "Changing Attitudes Toward a Merit Rating System." *Personnel Psychology,* 1955, *8,* 429–448.

ZANDER, A., and MEDOW, H. "Individual and Group Levels of Aspiration." *Human Relations,* 1963, *16,* 89–105.

ZANDER, A., and MEDOW, H. "Strength of Group and Desire for Attainable Group Aspirations." *Journal of Personality,* 1965, *33,* 122–139.

ZANDER, A., STOTLAND, E., and WOLFE, D. "Unity of Group, Identification with Group, and Self-esteem of Members." *Journal of Personality,* 1960, *28,* 463–478.

ZANDER, A., and ULBERG, C. "The Group Level of Aspiration and External Social Pressures." *Organizational Behavior and Human Performance,* 1971, *6,* 362–378.

ZANDER, A., and WOLFE, D. "Administrative Rewards and Coordination Among Committee Members." *Administrative Science Quarterly,* 1964, *9,* 50–69.

ZANDER, A., and WULFF, D. "Members' Test Anxiety and Competence, Determinants of a Group's Aspirations." *Journal of Personality,* 1966, *34,* 55–70.

ZYGMUNT, J. "Movements and Motives: Some Unresolved Issues in the Psychology of Social Movements." *Human Relations,* 1972, *25,* 449–467.

Index

Index

Index